to kiln

D1437173

XM 105

LABEL

ate

PLEASE TAKE CARE

OF THIS BOOK

GRACEMOUNT

The art of making pottery

from clay to kiln

GRACEMOUNT
SECONDARY SCHOOL
LIBRARY

Harry Memmott

Studio Vista London

©Paul Hamlyn Pty Ltd 1970-71
Published in London 1972
by Studio Vista, Blue Star House,
Highgate Hill, London N19

All rights reserved. No part of this
publication may be reproduced, stored in
a retrieval system, or transmitted, in any
form or by any means, electronic,
mechanical, photocopying, recording, or
otherwise, without the prior written
permission of the publisher.

Printed in Hong Kong by Lee Fung
Printing Company Ltd

ISBN 0 289 70306 9

preface

Harry Memmott is the grandson of a potter. To many, it would seem to have been quite natural that the grandson too should have gravitated to pottery. But although the grandson was brought up in the shadow of a kiln stack, and watched the work routines that he later was to practise, he was not a trained potter, nor even an apprentice potter, and the work he does now owes little to the grandfather.

'Grandpa' Sandison was a pioneer really – or to put it more accurately, a potter supplying pioneers. (It must be remembered Brisbane is a little over 100 years old.) Water did not often come through pipes and taps. Water was stored in large stoneware containers. The farmers stored their produce in large pots, big enough to contain two Ali-Babas. There were water jugs and milk jugs, and teapots and butter-coolers, all humble but very necessary items for hard-working people who could not and did not buy much pottery imported from overseas, except perhaps for Sunday best. Grandpa Sandison was certainly a unique character and Harry Memmott has certainly inherited this.

I had my pottery beginnings through Harry Memmott. Although he was not a potter at that time (about 1950), he introduced me to Mervin Feeney who was then a partner to Uncle George Sandison, who had inherited the pottery. It should be said that both Harry Memmott and I owe much to Mervin Feeney for his help, his encouragement, and for his link with tradition. He was a traditional potter in the Queensland manner. It is of added interest that this book shows many of these Queensland 'traditional' techniques. Mervin Feeney himself shows these techniques in some of the series of photographs on 'throwing'. These throwing techniques, developed through tradition, are captured in this unique series of photographs. But despite this help from Mervin Feeney, there was much Harry Memmott had to do alone for the times had changed, the dictates of fashion had bypassed the masters and there was even a new technology to be learned and added to the traditions. Harry Memmott built the first gas kiln in Queensland. The South Brisbane Gas Company drew a plan for him, and this was the forerunner of the dozens to follow.

In those days in Queensland there were no formal pottery courses and all of us had to borrow, beg and steal our knowledge from any source. There was hardly a book on pottery available in Queensland then, or none we knew about. But as there is a certain compassion and understanding between people suffering poverty, there is a sort of camaraderie between those trying to overcome a poverty of knowledge, and the best shared what they knew. And today those potters who pot in the relative safety of technical colleges and private studio schools can never really appreciate what it means to be offered this hard-gained knowledge so casually. They will never know, to the same degree, the despair and triumph from 'going it alone'.

Harry Memmott has said that if we owed much to Mervin Feeney, all of us learned a lot from each other. Our knowledge was gained more by dissection, rather than by explanation. If there is any benefit from this sort of education – with learning being spurred by necessity – it is that later when one becomes a teacher, not only can the wherefores be taught but also the whys.

If this book offers attitudes as well as techniques, it is as it should be. If it also serves to banish the mystique that for far too long has surrounded the subject, this too is as it should be.

There are now many books by potters, but not one of them is complete in itself. If this book offers anything different, as in fact it does, it is justified. I look forward to my copy.

Milton Moon
Ceramics Lecturer-in-Charge
South Australian School of Art
Foundation Churchill Fellow

acknowledgements

Without the original teaching by Mervin Feeney this book could not have been written. Most of the throwing techniques illustrated were demonstrated by this 'Master of the Wheel'.

The section on glazing was collated in co-operation with Milton Moon whose skill in this field is unsurpassed.

Oscar Hausknecht performed feats of gymnastic skill to snap, over shoulders and under arms, the potter's eye-view of work in progress.

Hours of patient collating and typing, as well as demonstrating were done by Liz Feldman.

Harry Memmott

11

introduction

This is a book on discipline, if personal discipline is a distasteful attitude, read no more – return this book to the shelf.

The discipline necessary will be the discipline of continued practice, until the article grows of itself, effortlessly and naturally, the mind being in harmony with the forces in use, the material and the design. Unlike some sporting disciplines which create an ability which fades as the body ages, the strength from this discipline will grow and the results will be of ever increasing interest for life.

Hamada, the internationally admired Japanese potter, is about seventy. My grandfather, James Sandison worked until he was past ninety, throwing works on the wheel that young men would find hard to equal in vigour and size. The minds of such men retain youthful zest and inquiry, and their natures reflect the balanced way of their lives. Their way of clay is actually a way of life.

This continuous attempt, along with the mystery of the fire, to capture spontaneous beauty fascinates the imagination, and the mind never grows weary of an adventure which has no ending. But this is only so if there is an understanding, not only of the technique of clay, but of the way of clay. Many promising students show great merit, then fade into oblivion. Having learned the technique, they find they have no knowledge of how to apply their knowledge. They are learned, but have little understanding of what they have learned. The master of language, who cannot write or talk; the critic of the arts who can do none of them; the general who knows the rules of war and loses every battle, and so on, are well known. All have an excellent knowledge of facts and even technique, but are unable to breathe life into any of it. So with clay.

The professional commercial potter, so adept on the wheel, has a knowledge and sympathy with his clay because it must be as near perfect as possible for him to do his work. But once he puts it on the wheel, although his technique is marvellous, the result is usually stilted. This is because it is at this point that imagination and design enter the scene and the commercial potter is usually acquainted with neither.

Usually commercial designs have been of the unimaginative ugliness which seems to be fairly universal in our society, particularly during the first part of this century – designs often conceived by someone who has never touched a piece of clay! This was less apparent in some small local potteries, their work having a naive approach suggesting the mediaeval pottery of England. For the most part, these potteries have now vanished from the local scene.

A similar attitude exists in the work of the small Asian potters who work for their village. Though these people have a different tradition and culture, they continue to create freely in their everyday work producing wares of great beauty. The artist-potter, a relative newcomer is often inferior in technique to the late wheel master of commercial pottery, but he has not been mentally dulled by the commercial approach of drab design and uniformity. He has a free attitude reflected in his work which is currently swinging to the extreme of individual design.

Many students begin pottery with a vague notion of aim. Some have the idea of imitating the most vulgar of commercial pottery. Others are swayed by the most avant-garde of contempory adventures. However, because of the initial demands of studying technique often their salvation is accomplished as they become aware of the nature of the material, its response to handling, and the subtle glazes of natural materials. Even the most vulgar acquires some taste and the would-be 'advanced' modern gains some depth instead of only superficial showmanship. Technique is the first hurdle. In the case of the potter's wheel, the ultimate quest is to have control of the clay with an ease which allows the mind to deal with the problem of form untroubled by the mechanics of making. This skill is achieved only by long practice, and a sympathy learned of the material and means. The doing can be done without thinking and the thinking is done of the form being made.

Each step of throwing on the potter's wheel will present its difficulties, but no difficulty is greater than the mastery of self. While this is being learned there will be black days of deep despair of ever making anything on this contrary rotating wheel. In some magical way, however, one day the problem will be solved as though the clay itself has suddenly decided to co-operate. The clay is no different, the wheel is the same – could it be the potter?

Sooner or later with practice of throwing, and learning to know the character and limitations of clay, a pot will grow. No worth-while results will come from strain. Knowledge of using the rigid bones to control the clay and the weight of the body to 'lean on it a little' and guide it on the path of obedience will aid towards ease of making. A touch typist learns to type without looking at the keyboard. Years later she can still type quite well, but without the slightest conscious knowledge of the keyboard. So with the potter's wheel. Having learned the basic techniques, restraint will fall away and the hands will seem to work by themselves. Eventually the potter will be surprised to find that the hands are performing movements as if of their own accord – working out the mechanics of a plan without conscious effort while the design seems to fully occupy the conscious mind.

Technique in handwork is similar. Experience will tell how far a slab of clay will bend, and which joins will remain joined and not crack. Anyone who has seen a native woman animatedly chatting to her friends while she nonchalantly welds coils to make a large jar, will have admired the speed and ease with which she works. The final result is a shape the same as that from the dark past of thousands of years, but the technique is magnificent. A certain quality of aptitude in hand building is necessary to assure ease of making, and confidence the piece will live through drying and firing to allow the mind freedom to consider form.

When a newcomer approaches with a partly formed and timid interest in clay, it is necessary to brainwash the brainwashing which various establishments have subjected the mind to over its formative years. Certain standards will have been proclaimed as the only standards. Commercial pottery will have made its claim for uniformity, and acceptance of its dullness with the boring aim of 'perfection'. There will be many blind worshippers of Asian work, English slipware tradition, contemporary avant-garde or primitive form and so on. This is of little importance. All such work should be studied but eventually judged by experience, not by conformity with dogmatic standards. It is natural that anyone living in a certain community will at first accept non-critically the dogmas of the environment. At a showing of any work which does not correspond to these pre-conceptions the eyes will not see and the mind will not accept. Acknowledgement would mean a shedding of comfortable standards (standards perhaps themselves so revolutionary not so long ago).

But how does a mind used to English floral patterned tea cups understand a Japanese tea ceremony bowl in its rough and crazed form with many imperfections? Is it possible for an admirer of German and Danish figurines of shepherdesses and dancing girls to view and admire roughly textured abstract slab clay sculpture? It takes a special talent to look upon the work of a man with a mind open to receive instead of judging without comprehending. The spectator should try to learn how to receive the message as the artist tried to impart it.

The mind of the clayworker, if it is to be creative, will of necessity view work from the past, because all art rests upon previous culture. Careful analysis will reveal that even what appears to be the most startling break in tradition is only a rational development from what came before.

While no potter will create original work by merely copying the work of the past, it is still a useful exercise. The purpose of such copying is not to create a slavish imitation but to learn from the problems of construction. That which appears to be straightforward may be found to be subtle.

Having tried to understand the mind of the mediaeval man who made that jug or the Asian who threw that teapot, and the difficulties they overcame, the next task is to store this knowledge in the reservoir of memory. There it can be used in the attempt to produce a contemporary creation.

Any original work will not be the result of strain, but of a natural and relaxed expression of what has been learned, digested and born as natural of today. Perhaps there may be some strain of body from working with concentration for some time, but if the result is even a little successful this is enough reward.

14

1

clay

The way of clay is to understand the nature of clay, its wonderful plastic response when handled with love and care, and its collapse and disintegration when maltreated, overworked and strained beyond its capabilities.

where to find the clay

The problem is to understand where to find it, how to select it, and then to prepare it for its function. If transport and muscles are available, enquiries will usually bring a flood of information about clay deposits. Everybody seems to know of a clay which should be good for making pottery. Even government departments will join in the game, with stories of old deposits which have never been used. From the clues which are available, particularly if they are from fellow potters, a search for suitable clay may be carried out.

Most good clay is some feet under the ground. Places where the earth has been sharply cut into, like cuttings or creek bends, will be where to look.

the properties of clay

What should you look for? The clay may look like clay is supposed to look, a white or red plastic mass, but then it might also be blue, tan, yellow, grey or black. If it is a shale clay, it might even look like rock. Take a small portion of what could be clay, wet it and knead it with the fingers to form a small sausage. Bend it. Try twisting it into a knot. See how far it will bend before it cracks. From this sample an idea of the plasticity can be gained.

The shale type of clay may have to be crushed and soaked for some time before this test can be performed on it. If the test seems satisfactory and sufficient quantities are available to make it worth-while to use, fill a bucketful and return to the pottery. Lay the clay out in a thin layer and dry it out. Break it into small pieces and add these pieces to water. It is well to form a habit in pottery of adding materials to water this is the easiest way to wet ceramic materials. Indeed, some materials will form a skin and not absorb water, if water is poured on them.

Sieve the slurry which has been made through a coarse screen, fine enough to remove objectionable material such as small stones, roots, leaves, and so on. Pour the slurry on to a porous surface such as a plaster-of-paris bat, and allow it to stiffen. Now mix or wedge it into a homogeneous mass. This process will be described later in this chapter. Make some shapes which would tend to slump, warp or crack, then make a shrinkage bar. This is a bar of clay about seven inches long, one inch wide and one-eighth of an inch thick. A plastic ruler with millimetres embossed on one side can be cut in halves so that the piece bearing the measure one-to-ten is retained and pressed into the clay bar.

When the piece is dry, the ruler can be compared with the now shrunken bar of clay, and the difference in millimetres is the percentage of air dry shrinkage. The bar can be compared to the ruler after the biscuit and glaze firings, a process which will be explained in detail later. The approximate shrinkages can then be estimated.

Experience indicates that the air drying shrinkage should be about six to seven per cent in a throwing clay and less in a hand building clay. The fired shrinkage for stoneware will be about the same. Unless fired in a 'perfect' kiln the fired shrinkage will vary slightly throughout the kiln. Therefore a bar must be placed in the hottest and the coolest parts of the kiln and the results must be averaged. With luck, the clay may meet all requirements and be a natural stoneware clay. The requirements for such a clay are availability, plasticity, strength, satisfactory drying, firing and glazing qualities and fired colour.

Plasticity and strength must be considered as two separate qualities. A highly plastic clay may be dug which will assume any shape. But it may have the unfortunate trait of slumping and being unable to support its own weight. Strength may be given to such a clay by adding a fire clay or a sandy type of clay, or any other type of clay which will not only complement the plastic clay and give it strength, but also assist to give the clay body – the remaining characteristics required.

Industrial potteries, using huge quantities of clay, blend a number of clays so that

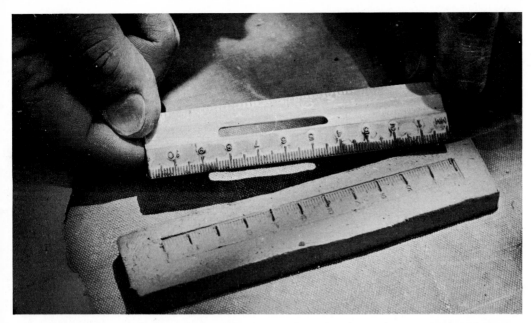

top: A prepared bar of clay has measurements imprinted upon it. It is compared with the ruler as it goes through the various stages of airing, drying and after the biscuit and glaze firing. Shrinkage is then gauged.

centre: Examples of short crumbly clay and a fat plastic clay.

bottom: Pieces of clay in the process of stiffening.

if there is any variation in the quality of any one clay of the batch, it will not radically alter the composition of the overall batch. If the potter personally selects the clay to be used, the question of consistency is less of a problem. The strata of clay will be obvious where it is being gathered. When clay is bought, however, it is best to buy before current stocks are exhausted and to run a quick test.

Do not make a clay body any more complex than necessary. Simplicity of ingredients means ease of compounding and more time for making. A simple clay body often has a quality which is lost in a complicated formula. The finer and denser the clay, the greater the difficulty of drying, and the more likelihood of warping and cracking. Most of these problems can be overcome with the addition of *grog* (ground firebrick of various mesh size) obtainable from a supplier of refractory products. The problem is to balance the non-plastic qualities of grog with the desirable high plasticity of the clay. Many potters prefer to add a sandy open clay which has some plasticity, to grog, which has none.

A highly plastic clay also has the disappointing quality of considerable shrinkage. It is wonderful to throw with a strong, highly plastic clay and to see what sizable things can be made. It is maddening to see the insignificant size that the same piece ends up, because of excessive shrinkage.

When stoneware pottery is fired and is required to *vitrify* (become glass-like) enabling it to hold fluids, even if unglazed, it must have a porosity of less than five per cent. If the clay body, on its own will not achieve this result the potter must add *flux* – that is material such as feldspar which fuses the clay particles. Not all stoneware is vitrified. Some Asian stoneware pieces are porous when made from sandy open clays.

With the advent of silicone, many potteries which have been troubled by leaky wares, now dip these pieces in silicone, sealing them completely. Feldspar is the most common ingredient used in the clay body as a flux, dissolving first the clay particles then the silica as the temperature rises, and forming the body into a vitreous mass. It is also a non-plastic in the clay body. Its purpose is to give vitrification and strength. Too much of it of course will cause deformation, warping and excessive shrinkage. The fired colour of the clay is controlled by the oxides in the clay, usually iron. Additions of other oxides and minerals can alter the colour as required.

Clay gathered locally gives the potter an awareness of the close relationship of earth and pottery.

Bought clay, highly refined by wholesale suppliers, is usually characterless. All the faults and impurities which give a clay personality have been removed. If the supplier has no sympathy with the use to which the potter is to put the clay, his supplies may be unreliable. From time to time the supplier may alter the source of materials without informing the buyer, or clumsy handling may adulterate the material. But, if a reliable, refined, powdered clay is available, the method of making a clay body is the same as with dug clay. Some character may be added to it with a rougher body, such as fire clay.

Summing up, if a clay is to hand which satisfies the potter's requirements, there is no need to go further. If the available clay is deficient in some factor, the missing factor must be added. Possibly a compound of materials will be necessary to form a clay body. As far as clay is concerned, very few types are pure, and it is only possible to generalize when describing them. Although the other minerals vary, they are constant enough in their essentials not to cause much concern.

The three main constituents of a clay body are: plastics, fillers and fluxes. Plasticity is given by the clay and will vary greatly with different clays. Fillers open the clay body, allow drying, and reduce shrinkage and warping. They are non-plastic. Fluxes cause the body to fuse into a solid mass and mature at a given temperature. Fluxes also act as fillers during air drying. The selection, and quantity of these materials, will depend on the type of ware to be made and the temperature at which it will be fired.

plastics

KAOLIN OR CHINA CLAY has low plasticity and dry strength. It has small shrinkage and is *refractory* (hard to melt).
BALL CLAYS are used for plasticity. They are fine grained and have a high dry strength. On their own they shrink excessively.
STONEWARE CLAYS have similar plasticity, but greater refractory characteristics.
FIRE CLAYS are refractory, some types are strong and plastic and very useful in a throwing body. They will assist with any drying problems.
BENTONITE is very fine grained clay used in very small quantities (about one or two per cent) to give plasticity.

fillers

SILICA, SAND, QUARTZ OR FLINT are non-plastic. They open the clay body to assist in drying and reduce shrinkage and thus prevent cracking. During the firing they act as 'bones' to the piece giving it the strength to retain its form without slumping, or reducing fired shrinkage.
GROG, crushed fired ceramic, has the same purpose.

fluxes

FELDSPAR, the most common flux, melts to bond the body together when fired.
NEPHELINE-SYENITE fuses at a slightly lower temperature.
LIMESTONE (WHITING) and talc are sometimes of use.

A throwing clay will be highly plastic and strong with emphasis on ball clay and fire clay for these qualities. For hand work and tiles the clay will need to be much more open and greater stress will be placed on fire clay and fillers. *Casting slip* (liquid clay for casting) will need less plastic qualities and kaolin and fillers will dominate.

equipment for preparing the clay

It is possible to buy fully prepared clay from a pottery supplier, or the local pottery or brick works. These days large potteries usually run their clay through a de-airing pugmill. This mixes the clay and removes the air from it by means of a vacuum chamber. This has the effect of making a clay of very even and plastic quality, requiring only kneading before use. If such a supply is available it will be a blessing.

If the clay has been pugged (mixed) in an ordinary pugmill, it is desirable to allow it to age for several weeks, before it will gain the qualities that a de-airing pugmill provides. After ageing it is better to knead or wedge the clay by hand rather than to pug it again.

Only the experience of success and failure can make it possible to judge the quality of the clay and to determine its use. Excess water from recent use, or air introduced from uneven mixing can cause cracking or bloating. Ageing or maturing is the answer to these problems. The clay must be well mixed. It can be stored as it comes from a pugmill, or if it is handmade, it should be wedged, preferably with a little old matured clay added to it. It should be stored in a warm, dank atmosphere in a container or under plastic. This allows for bacterial action to set in and expel air, causing the clay to become plastic.

Vinegar or a few drops of diluted hydrochloric acid in water added to the clay will assist to sour and mature the body. Do not be surprised if spiders, slugs and worms appreciate the same conditions that the clay does!

The importance of maturing clay may be judged by the great care which some Asian potters take to prepare clay for use by future generations. They are working with clay that their grandfathers prepared for them. The hand or foot wedging of clay is a process with obscure origins. The resulting smooth even body is only equalled by the de-airing pugmill of comparatively recent times. The process drives the air from the clay and mixes it to a homogeneous mass. It also reveals any foreign bodies that may have worked into the body of the clay.

Two differently coloured clays may be wedged to illustrate the mixing.

After the clay has been wedged twenty-one times it has over a million cuts through it, and becomes of even appearance and nature. Wedging is good exercise, and the use of the weight of the clay and flow of movement will help to take the hard work out of it. It seems easy until tried, but once this flow of movement is recognized it *is* easy.

Watch the surface of the cuts each time, and remove any foreign bodies that may have got into the clay.

Cut at least twenty-one times. After the trouble of wedging, do not allow the clay to deteriorate by lying it flat on any surface. Stand it on an edge so that the smallest-part possible is touching. When the clay is cut up for use leave the last thin strip on the table, as it will be uneven in texture after losing some of its moisture to the surface on which it was resting.

The potter's tactile and visual senses will tell him when the clay is just right for use.

When the clay has been wedged and has lain around for a while it may become crusty – the outside stiff and the inside soft. Kneading is used to recondition the clay to an even condition.

left: A vibrating sieve makes sieving easier.

top right: A mixer made from a forty-four gallon drum for mixing clay.

bottom right: A small pugmill makes the clay into a homogeneous mass.

wedging A

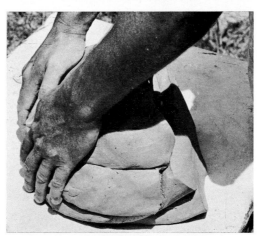

top left: Working on a damp plaster block or table beat the clay into a shape as shown. Resting it against the body, raise it enough to pass the wire under and vertically up through it.

top right: Place the cut ends towards the body and grasp one half of the clay with the palms rather than the fingers.

centre left: Swing the clay high and, using its own weight for momentum, strike it forcibly downwards on to the half on the wedging block.

centre right: Push the hands and fingers forward on the clay to the block.

bottom left: Pushing the hands forward causes suction which allows the clay to be lifted towards the body.

bottom right: Then turn the clay away from the body with the left hand, while your right hand moves towards the body. The clay is now back in its original position looking like a capital D, ready for the next cut and a repetition of the movements. Use the palm of the fingers to beat it into shape if necessary, and run the fingers over any surface cracks or marks.
Cut and wedge at least twenty-one times.

wedging B

top left and right, bottom left:
Illustrated is the wedging of two
differently coloured clays to show
how the clay is blended. The
wedging is handled as previously
described.

bottom right: After the clay has
been wedged twenty-one times,
it has over a million cuts through
it. The clay is now of an even
texture.

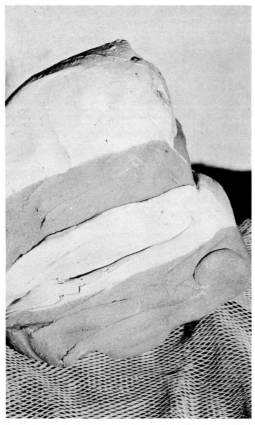

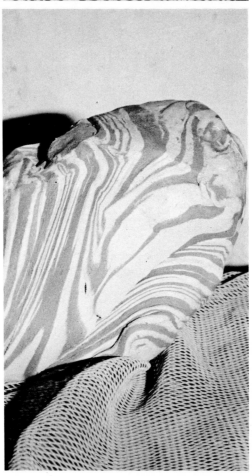

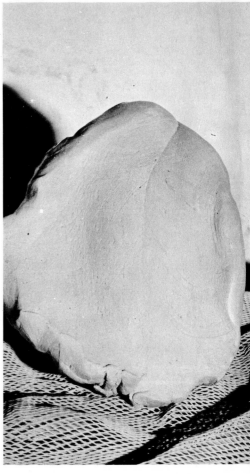

kneading

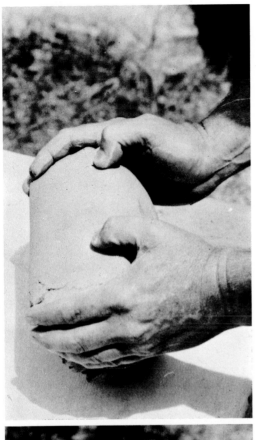

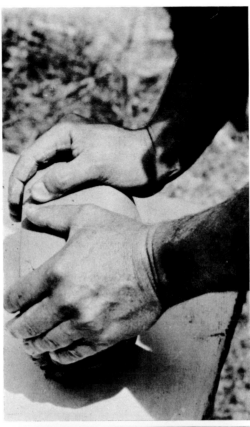

top left: The clay is placed on a plaster block. Kneading is done to freshen up a piece of clay which has been standing for some time after wedging.

top right: Hold the hands as illustrated and lean the body weight onto the clay while continually rotating the clay towards the body for a quarter of its circumference at a time.

bottom left: Press down with the heels of the hands while keeping the fingers at the ends of the clay to prevent spreading.

bottom right: As kneading progresses the clay will assume the appearance of a ram's head. By eventually reducing the pressure of the hands, the clay will revert to the rolled shape. Stand the clay on its end upon the block, and tap and rotate it to form a ball for throwing.

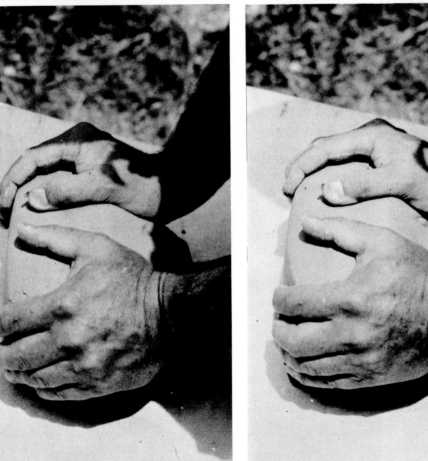

drying

Most ceramic pieces are lost during the air drying of the ware. Generally this is caused by a lack of understanding of the process plus the use of excessive water when making. Never use an excess of water. This is a common fault of pottery beginners.

Shrinkage, the cause of cracking, is equal in volume to that of the water evaporated. If the clay is saturated, particularly at the base which is always the slowest portion to dry, this is an invitation to cracking. Remove a piece off a wet bat as soon as possible and place it on a dry absorbent surface. Coarse-grained clay, like some kaolins and fire clays, shrink less than fine-grained ball clays. The coarse grains, or grog added to clay, allow the water to escape into the atmosphere. Fine plastic clays retain water. As the ware dries at the surface, the inside remains wet and the resultant strain causes cracking.

The potter has no option but to proceed carefully and slowly unless artificial means of drying are available. This is particularly true with large pieces. The larger the piece, the more non-plastics will probably be needed in the body. Industrial driers can be used to heat the ware quickly in a damp atmosphere. When the ware is thoroughly heated, the amount of humidity should be reduced. The artist-potter will probably compromise by air drying the ware and using the waste heat from the kiln to finish off the drying process.

The main drying problems are preventing the fine portions of the ware from drying too quickly (such as handles on jugs), and speeding up the slow drying parts (such as the base). The portions required to dry slowly may be wrapped in plastic. The slow parts can be dried by standing them on very absorbent surfaces or open mesh. As soon as possible the piece can be stood upside down or laid on its side.

Warping may occur during drying because of strain incurred during making, negligent handling, or uneven drying. The circular mouths of the ware can be kept round by using specially made forms, or old cracked bowls to dry on. Ensure that the curve of the piece used as a support is not too acute because the drying piece may shrink on to it causing cracking.

Tiles present a special problem. Each side should dry as evenly as possible. If one side is left downwards on plaster, the clay particles tend to accumulate tightly together on this surface. On the other side, they are much looser and this causes the tile to curl. The best technique is to dry a tile between two pieces of absorbent material, or on a mesh which allows air to approach each side. The tile should be turned several times during drying.

Bowl shapes can be cupped mouth-to-mouth to retain their shape. Air or sun can be a problem, causing distortion on one surface. When bowls are drying upside down the base tends to rise. If the base is convex, this makes the bowls into a top, or a 'spinner'. While the clay is still plastic, paddle it down slightly in the centre of the base and avoid this trouble. Certain shapes, may be found impossible to dry. The only answer is to alter the shape or to add non-plastics.

top left: Fast drying parts are restrained by the use of plastic.

top right: Vessels are placed on wooden slats or metal racks. This gives needed air circulation.

centre left: Large vessels which cannot be stood upside down are laid on their sides as soon as is practicable.

centre right: A mug shape is supported to prevent warping.

bottom left: Many repetitive shapes may be 'cupped' to retain their shape.

bottom right: Constant attention is needed if an infra-red gas heater is used in drying.

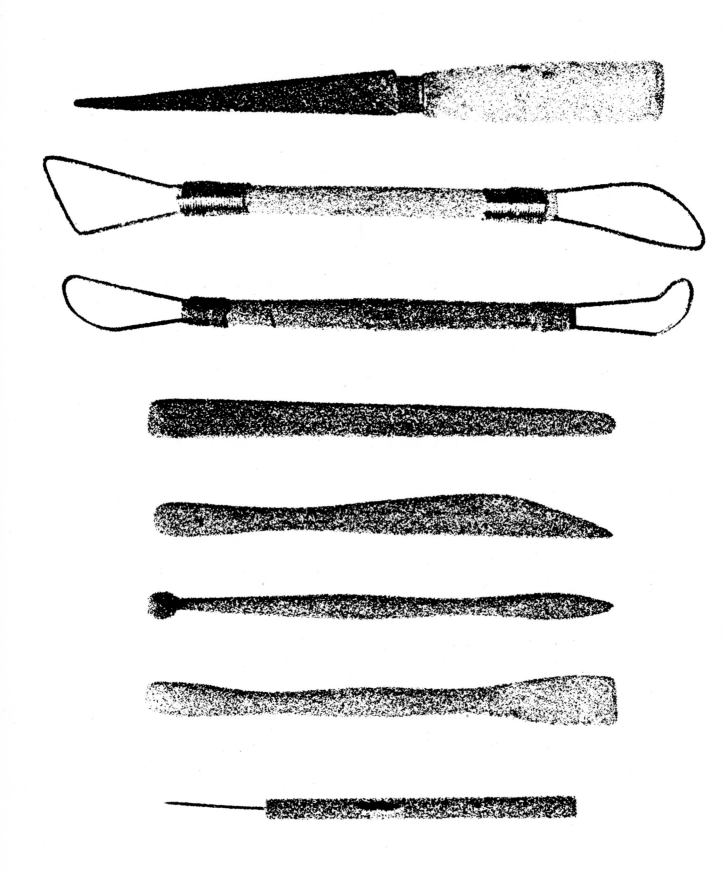

2

throwing
A. tools and techniques

Throwing on a potter's wheel is an art which the professional craftsman fully understands. The means and materials used are always the best available. A beginner will have enough problems throwing, without trying to use a wheel which has a jerky motion, or which wobbles from an insecure frame or light material structure.

wheels

A wheel should be chosen for its smooth running. It should have enough force or momentum to prevent the braking actions of throwing from stopping it easily. It should be built heavily enough to prevent it vibrating. Its driving mechanism and bearings should be big enough to keep it running evenly. Its speed should be about 0 to 150 revolutions a minute.

Some throwers favour *kick wheels* – that is wheels propelled by the foot. Kick wheels are certainly the easiest and cheapest to make and maintain. As the thrower has to provide the driving force, it is as well to be sure that kicking is not beyond the physical capacity of the person who is going to use it. In places where a ready-made wheel is available, price it first to see if it is really worth-while making one, providing of course the standard is high enough.

Kick wheels can easily be made by a handyman. The frame, drive shaft and bearings should be heavy enough to assure stability. The flywheel runs well if it weighs about 100 to 112 pounds. Rust proof materials are desirable for the tray. It must be built firmly enough to brace the forearms against without a feeling of insecurity. It should be rounded on the edge for comfort. The seat, if one is used, should be about level with the wheel and sloping slightly forward.

It is possible to convert the kick wheel into a power wheel by several methods. One which causes engineers to shudder, but which works well, is by the use of a slipping pulley belt. In these days of trade-ins, most of the parts required can be cannibalized from old washing machines. A long drive belt will be needed, and even a round industrial sewing machine belt will do, but a V belt is better. By the tension applied to this belt, the wheel can be driven at variable speed. Many other methods are used, but the beginner should do very well with one man power.

Construction of a power wheel always has the problem of how to obtain variable speed. One answer is friction wheels, where a small diameter wheel moves on the radius of a large wheel. Variable speed pulleys, cones which move and run one against the other, patent clutch devices, hydraulic controls, electrical controls, and other devices can also be used. Many of these are very expensive unless available from some disposal sale.

One of the cheapest is the use of the variable speed pulley. It must be a make which has a simple control lever, which, by some means, can be linked to and operated by a foot control. A reduction gear under the wheel head would be more compact than a large pulley, but much more costly.

To stop this wheel some electrical cut-out device must be linked with the foot pedal, or a first class waterproof switch attached to the side of the wheel. For any type of wheel a quarter to half horse power motor is sufficient.

The 'Zero Max' variable speed clutch is one of the simplest methods of reducing speed. The small size is adequate for throwing light balls of clay. For heavy work a higher torque may be required.

Hydraulic and electrical variable speed devices incorporated with the motor are available, but these are expensive. Most of the wheels in use in our pottery are of an old fashioned heavy industrial type, using a leather friction wheel passing over a larger wheel radially to vary the speed. Wheels using this principle will work very well as long as they are not too light. Small bearings and fragile friction wheels will not last long. It would be wise to obtain advice from a practising potter before buying a wheel.

Any light should be over, but slightly in front of the thrower to avoid working in one's own shadow. All switches should be waterproof, as a thrower's hands are always wet and covered with clay slush.

top: A kick wheel.

bottom: Electric potter's wheel (old friction drive type).

tools

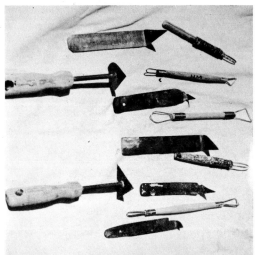

top left: For measurement of diameters, inside and outside calipers.

top right: Turning tools.

centre: These wooden tools have varied uses for finishing work.

bottom: Knives, tools for making holes and a scraper.

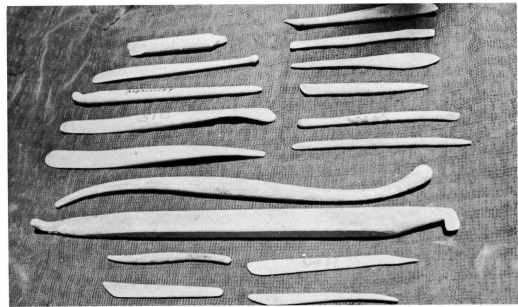

top: A long handled sponge is important for mopping excess water from narrow necked vessels.

bottom: Various throwing implements.

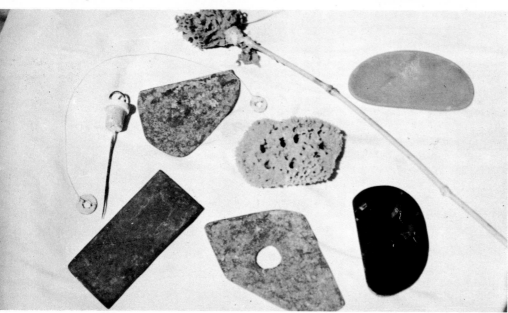

Throwing tools can be made from the simplest materials. To make a cutting needle sharpen a meat skewer, stick it through a cork, grind it to a fine point, and it is ready to use with a ring to hang it up by.

A wire cutter can be made with nylon fishing line, or piano wire tied to two bamboo nodules, washers, or whatever is handy.

Flat tools can be shaped from wood, metal or plastic. Flexible ones can be cut from shim steel, brass, or rubber.

Turning tools can be made from hoop iron and sharpened, or from wire or thin fret saws formed into a loop.

Sponges will be necessary. Flat sea sponges are useful for throwing. Cheap plastic ones are best for cleaning up. A sponge tied to a stick is needed to remove any water that may remain in deep cylinders where the hand cannot reach.

Calipers, inside and outside, are obtainable from hardware stores. Do not buy the type which screws up. The screw fills with clay and water, and soon will not work.

A small piece of leather or material is handy to round the rim. It will also quite easily become part of a pot if it is left lying around, and becomes attached to other clay.

For cleaning the wheel and bats a paint scraper is perfect. When throwing, the view of the potter is restricted almost to a plan view. An old mirror set behind the wheel will give a profile view.

making a bat

Wide diameter pieces are difficult to remove from the wheel head without distortion. Circular bats of some material are needed. Asbestos cement pieces, usually thrown away by builders, may be cut to a circular shape and used. A circle of clay is thrown on the wheel, and as long as it is wet enough to supply suction, the bats will stick to it. The bats should be slightly moistened so that they will not dry the clay circle hard, preventing adhesion. If the bat is too absorbent waterproofing may be necessary.

top: A circlet of clay is thrown to hold the bat.

bottom left: The bat is placed on the clay circlet.

bottom right: A smear of clay is put on the bat to hold the piece.

techniques of throwing

A bowl of water will be needed on the right side of the wheel. The soupier the water is with clay slush, the better lubricant it is, and the less likely to cause cracking in the clay. A good plan is to consider a throwing programme some days ahead if special clay is required. Very soft clay can be used to throw wide, flat plates. Firmer clay will be necessary for tall work. Thick ware should be well grogged.

With supreme optimism, the beginner will select clay to use with absolute disregard to its use or condition. Watch an experienced thrower carefully select the clay and then spend time preparing it to a perfect condition by wedging or kneading, after which the clay ball is shaped without flaws and of the correct weight for the size to be thrown.

Wedging not only removes the air from the clay it also seems to make it more plastic. No lumps, cracks or crusty surfaces are acceptable in the ball of clay about to be thrown. The ball of clay should be circular, with its ends flattened, something like a cheese. A crease left in the clay ball may remain on the pot bottom, creating a flaw which will develop into a crack later. Only sufficient clay balls should be made for immediate use, because the clay condition deteriorates quickly forming a crust on the outer surface. There should be no water or wet clay on either the clay ball or the wheel head as this will prevent adhesion.

Prepare the surface of the wheel to accept the clay ball by smearing some clay on it. The residue left when a pot has been cut and removed from the wheel is ideal to throw on. Under no circumstances throw the clay on a dry, dusty or wet, slushy wheel. In both cases, the surface may reject the clay ball and send it flying.

Adherence to the wheel is best obtained if the clay is thrown on to a moving wheel. If the clay lands off centre, stop the wheel, and try again or simply push the clay into the centre.

One school of potters in Japan has for many years deliberately thrown eccentrically off centre to give an individual character to their ware. This is a quality so many people, taught to accept uniformity and mathematical balance, are at a loss to appreciate. Before attempting to imitate such esoteric styles, however, the beginner would be advised to learn full control over the medium. The forces involved in centring must be considered. If the clay is moved towards the centre, centrifugal force will hold it there. As it moves outwards, the same force will throw it off the wheel. A fast speed will assist in centring, this same speed continued when the piece grows larger will probably cause its destruction.

A cone can be made on the wheel, with the wheel travelling at high speed. But if you pull the rim out to form a bowl at this speed, the result will be disastrous. It is most important to bear this in mind all the time. A fast wheel speed is best for centring gradually reducing as the pot nears completion. Large diameter bowls will be finished at the slowest speed commensurate with throwing.

There are different approaches to centring, but one thing all experienced potters have in common is that the clay is not pushed symmetrically to the centre. It would appear upon first consideration that the clay should be squeezed evenly on both sides. It will be observed in the photographs later in this chapter that this is not the case and that actually the clay is travelling under the hands in an eccentric form, owing to the way it is pushed. But when the hands are evenly removed, the clay is running perfectly in centre.

The arms must be braced, and held in a rigid manner to command the conduct of the clay. If the hands are moving from side to side during centring, the clay is the master and the thrower should stop and consider how to achieve authority over the clay. Rest the forearms on the side of the splash tray, or brace the elbows into the sides of the body.

If strength was the only power necessary to centre, potters who make hundreds of pieces a day would be physically exhausted long before the day's end. If very large pieces are being made, strength is required. But for most pieces, the weight of the body leant forward, with the arms rigid, is sufficient to centre the clay.

One method of centring is to push the clay away from the body with the heel of the left hand against the movement of the wheel, while the fingers of the right hand are used to pull the ball of clay towards the body. A larger ball of clay may be easier to centre is you extend your left hand past the centre of the wheel, and directly away from your body, while your right hand braces your left and shapes the ball of clay. Squeezing the clay so that it rises up and then pushing the ball down again will improve its condition if repeated a few times. Some throwers centre the clay into a high conical mass then force the hand to open it up.

The style shown in the illustrations in this chapter centres the ball about one and a half times as wide as it is high. This allows the base to be finished immediately by pressing the thumbs down into the centre of the clay until the correct thickness of the base is reached. Use a needle to ascertain the correct thickness if necessary. Do not plunge the needle into the centre of the base but to one side. The centre is harder to heal. Experience will soon make this test unnecessary.

problems of throwing

The beginner's way can be thorny. Even an experienced thrower has periods of error when nothing will go right. Here are some of the common troubles which most beginners encounter.

1. The beginner has an optimistic attitude that any clay in any condition is suitable to throw with. Only a skilled thrower can competently handle short or weak clay, and would never throw with clay improperly wedged or kneaded. The beginner blissfully ignores that which the expert insists upon.

2. Do not use excessive weight of clay to attempt a shape. Throw with the minimum amount of clay to improve technique.

3. Correct centring is essential for symmetrical work. In normal throwing the clay must be truly centred in the early stages of throwing.

4. Cracking is usually caused by the use of too much water. Lubricate the hands with clay slurry rather than water. Do not throw water on the pot. Do not allow water to form a pool inside the pot.

5. Remember to brace the arms rigidly when centring. If the hands are moving in an erratic way, the clay is in control – not the thrower.

6. Use slow rhythmic movements of the hands. Do not release the hands from the pot abruptly. Drawing up the walls too quickly in relation to the speed of the wheel will also spiral the wall and make the rim uneven.

7. Keep even pressure on the walls while drawing up. Usually the inside and outside pressures are applied opposite one another, however when drawing up, the outside hand can be under the inside.

8. Do not be too long in making the basic shape. Clay suffers from fatigue and will collapse.

9. Control the top edge constantly. Keep the rim thick until the completion of the shaping. This will give the rim strength and stability.

10. Do not make a shape which will slump either just after making or during the firing. (See illustration *page* 36).

11. Join the thrown accessories such as handles and spouts as soon as possible. Do not forget to trim the body of the pot if it is too heavy.

12. Allow for firing shrinkages and glaze thicknesses. If a lid has to fit into a neck, there are several layers of glaze to contend with.

13. Consider the relationship of the body to the wheel before starting. Do not place yourself in an awkward position. Have all the necessary tools and materials to hand. Be above the wheel if possible.

14. When cutting the pot off the wheel head, keep the wire down hard on the wheel Cut away from the body.

15. Use the needle to test the thickness of the base. Try to keep the base and the bottom of the wall thin, and retain clay near the rim to be used as the pot develops. (See illustrations *page* 37).

16. When drawing clay out on the wheel to form a flat plate, do not take it too far and cause a collapse as the clay supply runs out. Stop before this happens and draw up the sides. (See illustration *page* 36).

17. If a tool is being used, make sure that it is done to maximum advantage. For

instance, a flexible tool should fit the curve, not just touch a segment of it. (See illustrations *page* 35). A needle should be held rigidly when trimming a rim. Be precise when using calipers and make sure the measurement is as it should be. Do not make a lid too large or too small to fit the bowl through faulty measurement.

18. Finally but most importantly the thrower's approach should be one of total empathy with the piece at hand. The body should not be in a condition of locked rigidity, too stiff to even move, or have the sloppiness of a body without bones. It should be braced to force the clay's obedience without losing the fluidity of movement, or becoming tired from tension. A clear idea of intent should be held, with a plan of the sequence of movements needed to make the piece.

top: Here a flexible tool is used correctly. The full edge is curved to fit the shape.

bottom: This tool is being used badly, as only part of its edge touches the pot.

top: Do *not* choose a shape that will slump.

bottom: Or bring a plate so far out it will collapse.

practice exercises for throwing

top left: Push thumbs into the ball of clay.

top right: With flowing movement open ball out.

bottom left: Push it back in.

bottom right: Now draw it up . . .

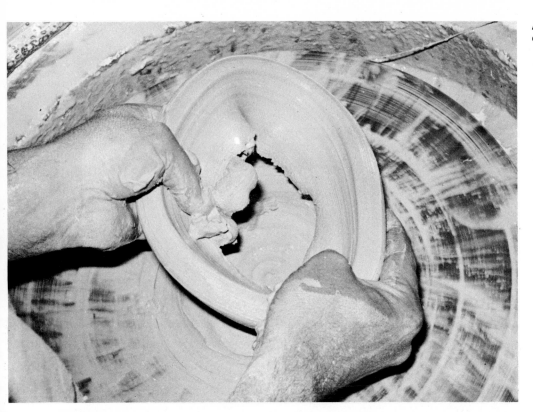

Beginners to throwing tend to defeat their own efforts because of timidity. Before commencing throwing, loosen up with this exercise. Make a few balls of clay of varying sizes, take one and centre it. With flowing movements and without pause, push the thumbs into the ball of clay. Keeping a strong roll of clay at the rim, open the ball out; push it back in; draw it up; and open the top. In other words, play freely with the clay, without restraint. Observe what the clay will do. When it falls apart, notice how it does so and how long it takes. The aim is not to make a pot, but to gain confidence and rhythm of work freely and without effort. Playing with several balls of clay like this will give the feel of the clay, and take away tension.

Now try making a series of predetermined shapes. Keep at it until the shapes are as close as possible to the idea. Take some balls of clay of the same weight. Throw a cylinder as high as possible, or a bowl as wide as possible – then slowly reduce the weight of the clay ball while still attempting to stretch the clay to the same size. It is amazing how much clay will be discovered, especially near the base of the pot. Cut the shapes in halves to see which parts can still be thinned.

Use various clays, so that the nature of different clays can be compared. Practise several days with a short, unresponsive clay. Then use strong, plastic clay, and find how battling with poor clay to make it behave has been instructive. You will feel the delight of a very detectable advance.

Attempt using less and less watery slurry on the hands as a lubricant. Most beginners use far too much water, causing cracking. If the aim is to make functional pottery, throw a series of beakers, bottles, or similar repetitive shapes exactly the same. Measure the clay, and follow a pattern of hand movements in precisely the same motions. Repeat it many, many times.

Recognize a pattern of movement. Centre the clay, then throw with the eyes shut, relying just on feel – not just of the thickness of the clay wall, but of the flow of the clay passing through the hands. When a sloppy movement is made, reread the tried approach as described here, and see if this helps. Have someone ask for a description of movements in the making of a certain shape and then try and consider each distinctive move and change of action.

Once these basic moves are clear in the mind, throwing becomes much easier. Practise them in the air at odd times. When the throwing requires no thinking, the technique has been acquired, and the mind can concentrate on design. But that will be after much practice, practice, practice.

turning and finishing

top: The bowl is placed on a wheel, or special head as here. The clay should be leather hard.

centre: The bowl is tapped until it runs truly centred. That is, if the forefinger is held near the rim, the bowl passes at an even distance whilst rotating and is concentric. If the bowl is on a wheel several plugs of clay may be used to hold securely after centring.

bottom: Any excess weight is turned off the bowl. To do this the turning tool is held very firmly in one position, so that the high spots of the bowl are gradually removed and the sides are evenly rounded. If the turning tool is not rigidly held, the faults in the bowl will dictate the movement of the tool and emphasise any inaccuracy.

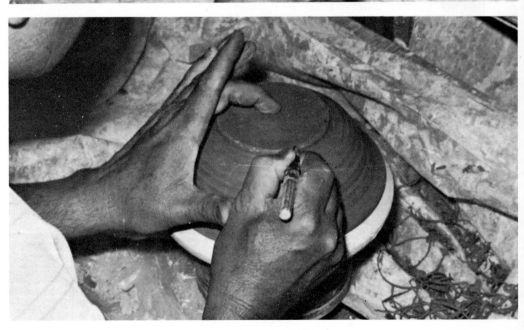

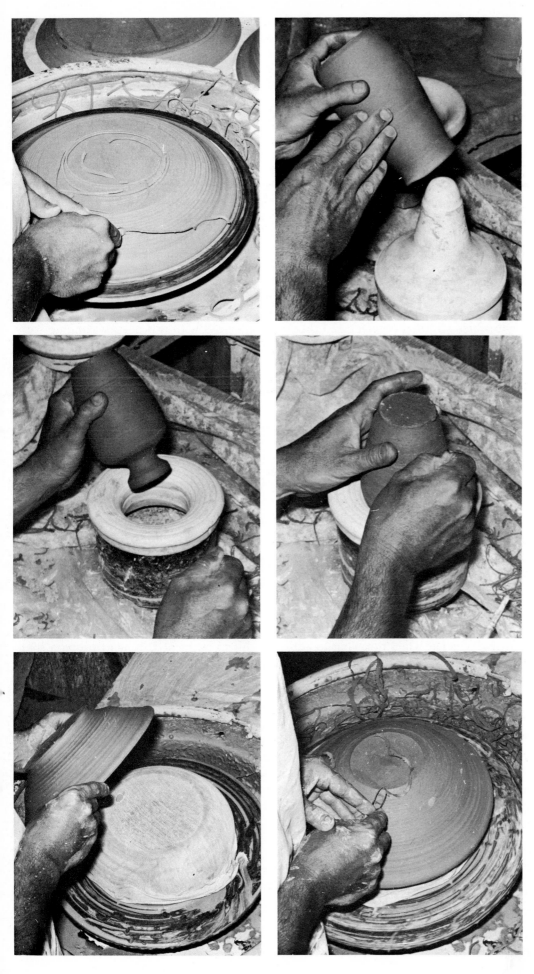

top left: When turning a wide, flat shape on the wheel it will probably not need to be supported.

top right, centre left and right: Special chucks may be used for pieces to be placed over or in for turning.

bottom left and right: A block of clay thrown on the wheel can form any of these chucks. A cheesecloth cover will prevent adherence.

After a pot has been thrown, it may be necessary to thin its walls.

The piece is allowed to harden, care being taken that it is not exposed to air or heat unevenly so that one side will dry more than the other. When the clay is of a heavy cheeselike consistency, and strong enough to be handled, it is known as leatherhard. This degree of stiffness for turning will vary. A large flat plate will have to be quite stiff, or it will flop while handling. A bowl which needs to have a handle attached, or to be beaten into a shape will be much softer. The ideal state for this process is when the clay peels off in long even rinds.

Various tools are used. They include loops of wire or fine saw blades on a handle, metal hooks made from hoop iron or ready made tools from the suppliers. Brass tools are useless for this process because they will wear too quickly. Fine fret saw blades bent round and onto a handle and then bound are efficient and cheap. Flat tools must be kept sharp. Turning can be done on the normal head of a potter's wheel as in the following illustrations:

Practice will be needed, so keep all pots initially for turning practice. If in doubt as to whether the pot is centered, hold a finger near the edge. If the distance between the rotating pot and the finger remains even, then the piece is running true. If not, the pot is either not centred or out of shape. There may be the occasion when one part of the pot is definitely out of line with another. A decision must then be reached as to which will be accepted, and the piece is centred with this portion running truly. The wheel should travel at a good speed. The tools must be sharp and rigid. A selection of files will be necessary for sharpening, as the clay blunts edges quickly.

Hold the turning tool firmly with a braced arm. Do not follow the surface of the piece. The tool should slowly approach the wall, taking off high spots and only then begin to turn the main wall of the pot. If the piece is not quite circular, after turning for a while and then stopping the wheel, it should be possible to observe that the high spots are being cut into, and the low spots are untouched. If this does not happen, the tool is being held too loosely and the hand is being controlled by the uneven surface. It is best to aim at throwing pots which do not need turning. This is most unlikely to be possible for some time, but mastery of the clay will never be gained if the thrower depends on turning.

Some pots will be deliberately thrown thickly to facilitate the shaping of the pot in planes, ridges or other designs, or making shapes virtually impossible by normal even throwing.

The base of the pot is usually left flat in stoneware. Practice should make it unnecessary to turn, although a hit with a paddle on the centre of the base will make sure the piece sits firmly. Some potters use a twisted cutting wire (usually made by plaiting three strands together) to cut the pot from the wheel head, leaving a characteristic pattern on the base of the pot. If a foot is desired, that is a ring of clay on the base, a little extra clay is left when throwing to allow for this to be turned. When turning a shape where it is impossible to feel the thickness of the clay to check it, tapping the surface and becoming used to the sound and feel will give the answer. Where the body is of coarse ingredients and a smooth surface is required, a soft kidney-shaped rubber is used, this will press the surface smooth. A sponge removes the fine and exposes the coarse particles so making the surface rougher. A flat steel edge on a fairly dry surface will expose the grog and cause cavities to give a rough finish.

Many potters use slip to brush on or dip the ware into, to give smooth finishes which are often coloured. This is a matter of taste, and the piece itself should suggest whether it needs a smooth or rough surface. Check any pieces which must fit. Lids will have shrunk slightly faster than the main body but if, when thrown, a lid was on the large size, now is the time to shave a trifle from it. Turning must be done in sympathy with the clay. A shape may be turned from a live thing into a hard mechanical nonentity. When a pot is turned it tends to lose the character of direct throwing. The appearance is of tool cutting, not the softer surface more subtly made by the fingers. Even the feel of the pot is different. Examine the shape carefully. Let it speak. Do not dictate to it.

B.throwing actual shapes

throwing a cylinder

The cylinder is the greatest challenge to the would-be potter on the wheel. Much practice is necessary to persuade the clay to defy gravity, grow slowly higher and yet to keep the walls evenly thin. Here it is demonstrated by a professional potter with quick precise movements perfected from years of practise.

Speed is essential when making a piece of height, as after a time the clay becomes fatigued from an excess of handling which causes the sides to slump, and the cylinder to lose height.

top left: The ball of clay is centred, with the ball being about one-and-a-half times as wide as it is high.

top right: The thumbs are pushed into the centre of the clay and pointed slightly towards the body. The arms are braced rigidly on the side of the wheel tray or against the sides of the body. The hands surround the clay and the right thumb pushes towards the little finger of the right hand while the left hand steadies.

centre left: A bowl shape develops. Widen the bottom making sure it is the correct thickness. Test with a needle if unsure.

centre right: The outside is gathered to the approximate diameter of the base. The bottom is now slightly larger in diameter than it will be when finished. Now think of the clay as if it were a stick that is being picked up with the thumbs back towards the little fingers for a start, and ending up opposite the centre of the hand.

bottom left: In one smooth movement a cone is drawn up. Put pressure on with the thumb, and with the heel of the left hand pressing towards the centre of the wheel, the clay rises to a conical shape.

bottom right: Open the mouth of the cone to permit a hand to fit inside by putting two or three fingers of the hand into the mouth of the piece. Let the clay run up between the small finger of the right hand and the second smallest finger, right up to the knuckles as shown. Let the clay run up between the thumb and forefinger of the left hand, and steady the clay as the mouth is opened.

top left: It is worked up again to required thickness. The middle finger of the left hand, being the longest, will go to the bottom of the cylinder. Then with the right index finger braced with the other finger and thumb try to feel through the bottom wall of the cylinder for the finger pressing out from the inside.

The left thumb is used to brace against the knuckle of the right forefinger. The clay is now allowed to ride up steadily. Keep the mouth of the cylinder narrow. The wider it gets, the less control there is over the clay. Try to draw the clay as high and narrow as possible.

top right: The piece is not quite a cylinder yet, it is hollow in the centre, slightly wider at the top and still wide at the bottom, with the bottom walls still a little thick.

bottom: The rim is steadied. The fingers of the left hand are inside the cylinder, the thumb outside. The middle finger of the right hand is on top of the rim, the second smallest finger pressing slightly on the outside. Do not let the top of the rim run dry. Only dampen the hands, do not throw water on the clay.

top: The excess clay is removed from the base. As there is slightly too much clay at the bottom of the cylinder, remove it now with the finger or a tool.

centre: A final drawing up removes the lipped shape of the rim and it becomes a true cylinder. Put the left hand down as far as possible into the cylinder feeling through with the middle finger of the left hand from the inside and the fingers of the right hand from the outside. Press again, keeping a little more pressure on the right hand than on the left hand, otherwise the cylinder will get too wide, and as the aim is height not width, keep it narrow. Do not try to lift all the clay from the bottom with one lift, this will weaken the clay. Try to lift two or three times.

bottom: Here in the final stage the rim is trued.

Once a cylinder with its height twice the diameter is thrown the essentials of this most important exercise are being mastered. At this point it is of interest to consider a fast professional throwing a flower pot. This thrower (now superseded by a machine) could make three four inch pots a minute, hour after hour, for perhaps nine or ten hours a day, in our recent past. Now obviously centring was not done as a laboured procedure as described. It was part of a rhythmic flow of production. Note the word rhythmic. A rhythm of work gives a steady output indefinitely continued. Often what appears a slow pace results in a large volume of production at the end of the day. But pottery throwing does not even look slow in this type of work — and it is not.

The process of centring for this speed production is actually done as the pot is being drawn up. As soon as the ball of clay hits the wheel the thumbs were forced into it. No time was lost centring as a separate motion. The hands gripped the clay, pressing in a clockwise motion as the cylinder was raised as described.

The right thumb had put a hole in the base, levelled the base, and discovered the correct thickness for the side. The clay ring was extended slightly with this pressure still on it, then pressed slightly inwards to give the walls of the pot a sharp angle from the base. The clay was quickly drawn up to a cone, then made into an inverted cone to make a flower pot. Why should this industrial procedure interest the artistic purist? The industrial potter, from time who knows when, has arrived at those movements which are easiest and quickest for the job in hand. For any thrown work, the quicker one can arrive at the basic shape, the longer can be spent on finishing the shape. An overworked shape must be either very thick and heavy or collapse.

The old potters took a pride in the quality and speed of their work, and the descriptions given here are of a dead craft as the machine now makes many of the pieces, and moulds make the others. High speed mass produced hand thrown pottery is a thing of the past, fortunately here are the photographs and descriptions of these skills so that the slower more thoughtful art potter can study them.

throwing a large bowl

top left: Throwing large pieces requires skill and strength. The technique is to use the hands rather than the fingers. Here a highly skilled commercial thrower has centred a piece of clay about ten pounds in weight, and has made it about four inches high.

top right: The heel of the left hand is forced into the clay with the arm very stiff, and the right hand steadying with the fingers on the outside of the clay. Note how the arms are bracing one another, and a strong clean rim is kept on the clay.

bottom left: The ball of clay has been hollowed out, and as soon as the thickness of the bottom is established, the clay is forced outwards to slightly more than the finished width of the bottom. The right hand is still steadying the left.

bottom right: The clay is gathered inwards to the approximate finished diameter of the base.

opposite—
top left: With one smooth movement the clay is lifted up into a cone twelve or fourteen inches high.

top right: Both hands grip the top rim firming and truing the clay, making the mouth of the cone wide enough to admit the right hand.

bottom left: The excess clay near the base at the wheelhead is removed, and pressure is applied radially inwards.

bottom right: The right hand is now placed inside, and the left outside, applying pressure almost evenly from both sides.

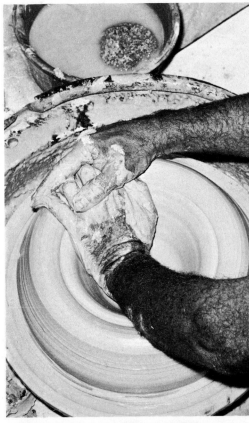
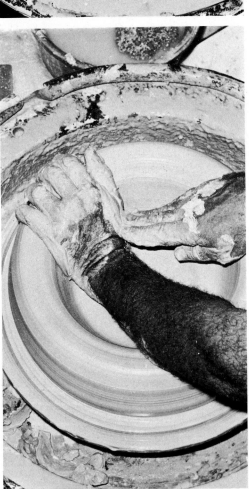

throwing a large bowl

top: The shape is drawn up and the top is narrowed.

bottom left and right, opposite top left: The position of the hands is now reversed. The left hand is inside and the right outside. More pressure is being exerted outwards than inwards, as further height and shape are developed.

opposite top right and bottom: The shape is refined and trued.

throwing a large bowl — basin shape

top: The large ball of clay is run true before centring. When throwing a large ball of clay, carefully prepare it into an even ball. Have it running as true as possible before attempting to centre. Brace the arms and body well. Use the hands as shown in almost a braking action in order to really shape the clay into the centre rather than force it. The method used with the heel of the hand to open the ball of clay is for balls over about eight pounds in weight. Weaker people would probably open best by pushing out with the right hand and supporting with the left. The hand positions are merely reversed for the next three photo descriptions.

centre: In this case, the clay is being pushed down with the ball of the left hand near the thumb, with the fingers curved around touching the outside of the ball of clay. The arm is held rigid. The right hand is bracing with the fingers.

bottom, opposite top left: The ball is gradually opened down and out. At this point the base is as thick as it will be when finished. The pressure of the left arm is downwards rather than outwards while opening.

top right: Now the hands move to the outside of the piece, bring them together slightly. The diameter and thickness of the base should now be about correct. A fat roll of clay is on the top edge of the piece.

bottom: The clay is then brought up into a cone, by the left hand as described for the making of a cylinder.

53

top: Open the mouth of the cone, keeping the roll of clay on the rim.

centre: As with the cylinder, the shape is brought up from the bottom. The middle finger of the left hand goes to the bottom, with the thumb over and steadying the rim. The right hand presses from the outside – its knuckle opposite the longest finger of the left.

bottom, opposite top: The clay is then drawn up, but outwards instead of inwards. Draw up only as much as can be managed at a time. The wheel should now be turning slowly. Remove any 'rags' near the base, then draw out to the finished shape.

centre: Steady the top. With this type of bowl, the wider and shallower it is, the slower the wheel should rotate and the greater care must be shown. One wrong movement and the lot will collapse. Large bowls of any size a thrower is capable of can be made with this method.

bottom: Cut-through view of the development of the shape.

throwing a shallow bowl

top left: As this article will be difficult to lift up on completion without distortion, it can be thrown on a bat. Centre the clay.

top right: Draw up but do not cone the clay inwards.

bottom left: Draw the sizes directly to the form, by opening out to small cylinder.

bottom right: Proceed to thin the clay as previously described. Remove any waste from the outside edge near the bat before the projecting sides make this difficult.

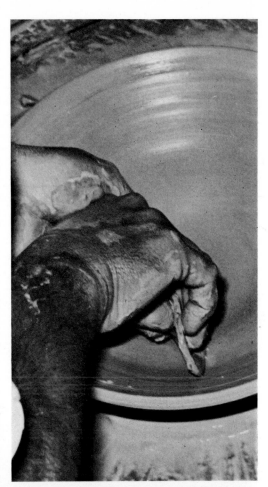

top left: True the top edge. The bowl is now at correct thickness, but for this example too deep. Observe the constant attention to the top edge.

top right: Use a flexible rubber to shape the inside of the bowl.

bottom: Now use very slow speed. Carefully finish the shape. Round the edge. Cut between the bowl and the bat. Remove the bat from the wheel by gentle levering up with a strong piece of steel. Do not use one of the turning tools.

throwing a flat plate

top left: In this instance centre a ball of clay about three pounds weight so that when centred it measures about six-and-a-half inches in diameter and about one-and-a-quarter inches high. This is achieved by pressing the edge of the right hand down on the top of the ball of clay to flatten it, whilst keeping the left hand pressing slightly on the outside of the clay ball, stopping it moving out of true, and giving the required shape.

top right: The grip is now changed and the heel of the left hand is pressed on the centre of the clay, the arm being quite straight, braced from the shoulder. Steady with the tips of the right fingers, pressing down to flatten the clay. At the same time let it go outwards, bending the tips of the left fingers into the edge to stop wobbling.

bottom: Continue this movement until you have a flat pancake of clay on the wheel, of a thickness near that desired.

top left: To gather the edge, the hands are placed on the outside edge of the clay, the thumbs on top. Pressing with both small fingers towards the centre of the wheel, gather the clay and turn the edges up.

top right: Remove the 'rag' of clay on the outside of the piece against the wheel, using the tip of the finger or a tool. This possibly eliminates the need to turn the foot.

bottom: Curving the outside edge. Bring the tips of the middle and second and smallest fingers of the left hand inside the rim, pressing outwards slightly against the support of the right index finger, curving the side into the required shape. Keep the thumb of the right hand on the edge to keep it true.

throwing a flat plate—a different technique

top left: Centre the clay by locking the hands together and press against the motion of the wheel with the left hand. Steady and shape the clay with the right hand into a flattish form. The arms must be kept stiff.

top right: Keeping the right hand performing the same task, place the heel of the left hand in the centre of the clay and press downwards to make the finished thickness, as this is accomplished moving both hands outwards.

bottom: Continue this movement until the bottom of the plate is finished, reducing the wheel speed as the diameter of the plate grows, as the speed of any point on the growing diameter is increasing rapidly. The ring of clay taken out to the circumference is kept true and steady by the manner in which it has been held.

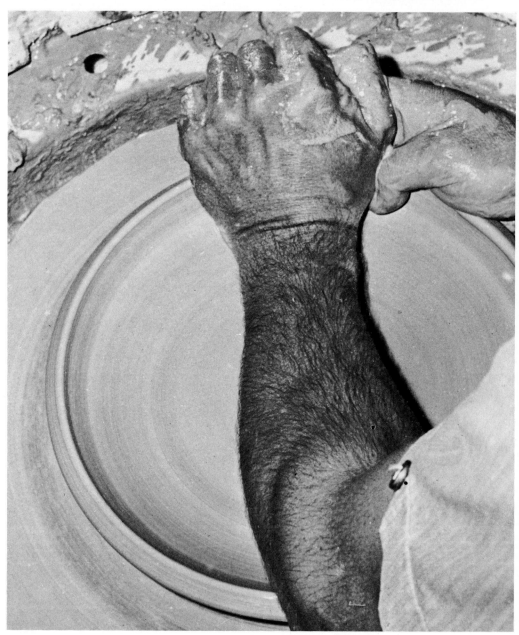

top left: Bring the hands back, bracing the elbows against the body. Keep the wheel speed low. Remove any rough clay near the wheel with a finger or tool. Press down and outwards with the middle fingers of the left hand against the index fingers of the right hand. At the same time the edge is controlled with thumbs, left forefinger and hand.

top right: The plate may be smoothed with a flexible steel or rubber tool. Keep the elbows braced to the body and the hands together on the tool. Do not take the tool left of centre in such a way that it will plough into the clay now rotating against it.

bottom: Polish the edge and round it with a piece of leather, plastic or similar material.

Observe how the movements in this series concentrate on using the arms as a locked form. The elbows keep against the body when possible. The fingers work as flexible tools on the stiff arms. A weak person will find this a satisfactory method of working, as the form is made with the stiff bones rather than strong muscle. As this article is shown being made on an asbestos cement bat, the clay can be fairly soft, and easy to handle as the form is practically fully supported.

throwing a lidded vessel

This shape is generally used for cooking or storage. The bowl is thrown as previously described.

top left: As the wall is thinned and raised, a fat ring is retained at its top.

top right: The base is finished to correct thickness and to its approximate diameter. For control over the clay the rim is kept a smaller diameter than finally required.

centre left and right: The vessel is drawn up slightly over the desired height and the rim is now shaped to accept the lid. It is still kept smaller than its final diameter.

bottom left and right: The belly of the pot is now made, as the clay is extended the correct height is attained, and this time measured for the lid size with inside calipers. Some potters work to a number of standard sizes for lids. This enables easy replacement if either part of the vessel is destroyed.

top: Finish the surface of the vessel as usual with a plain or decorative surface. If the vessel is for cooking, deeply inscribed decorations will be difficult to clean.

centre: It may be necessary to remove some excess clay from the bowl. This is done by centring the leather-hard bowl on the wheel and gently tapping it until it is running quite true.

bottom: Keeping the arms stiff, trim off the excess clay. Tap the centre of the base a little in, or turn some from it so that the pot will rest on the outer edge, and not spin on a raised point in the centre.

top left: If the lid is to be flat a strong clay is desirable.

top right: Pull out a flat plate form leaving a thick base on the wheel.

centre left: Outside calipers, with the same setting as the inside calipers used to measure the bowl rim, can now be used to gauge the width of the lid.

centre right: Shape the knob of the lid as much as possible, and scribe a line where it will be cut off, with the needle.

bottom: Encircle this line with the cutting wire, crossing the wire and pulling to separate the lid from the wheel.

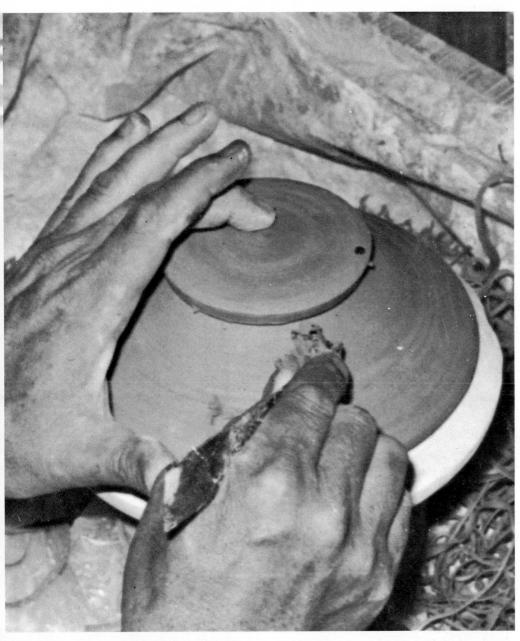

Should the vessel be used to cook or convey hot food, handles or lugs may be attached. One way to do this on the wheel is as follows.

top left: A small ball of clay is opened out into a ring, leaving a depression in the centre.

top right: The ring is shaped so that it will have flanges around its base.

bottom left and right: Scribe a line at the base and then cut away with strong wire.

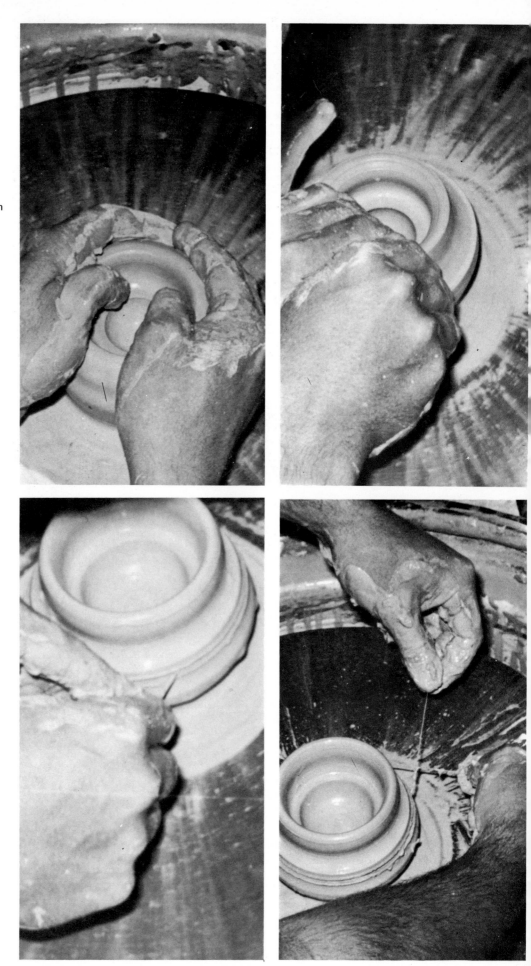

If the bowl is leather-hard it may be necessary to score the surface. If the clay is just firm this is not necessary. Some slurry may be put on the surface of the bowl where the handle is to be attached.

top: Adhere the lug by moving it slightly from side to side to induce suction and exclude air, fixing its position and keeping it level.

centre and bottom: With the left band supporting the inside of the vessel, firmly press the flange, welding the lug to the body.

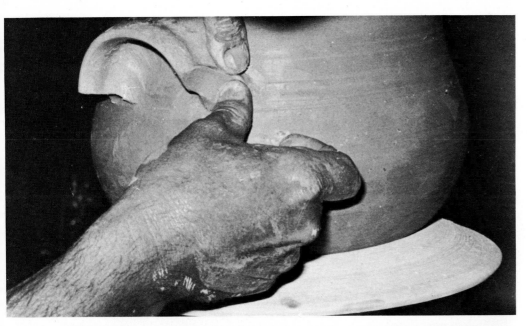

top: Adhere the ends of the lug, removing sharp corners and shaping during the process. Line the other lug up and repeat the process. It is easy to line up for height as the pot can be viewed in profile. If difficulty is experienced placing the lugs directly opposite one another, a ruler placed on top of the bowl will help. When firing the type of vessel described, its lid may be fired on it to prevent warping as described in Chapter 7 on Glazing.

bottom: The vessel is now finished.

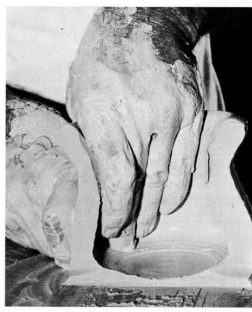

top left: Cross-sections of stages in the development of the bowl of the lidded vessel.

top right: Cross-section showing finger movements in drawing up the bowl.

bottom: Finished piece in section.

throwing a narrow necked bottle

The technique is similar to throwing a bowl as just described.

top left: Start with the bowl shape as previously described but it is not drawn up as high as the previous shape, the bowl at this point being half the height of the piece.

top right: A lot of clay is being kept at the top half of the shape, whilst the bottom half is being completed. Remove any water.

opposite bottom, top left and right: The jar shape is obvious and the neck is now being thinned and narrowed with clawlike pressures, and by pressing with the left fingers inside, left thumb outside.

bottom: Now a neck shape is beginning. True the top edge. Pay constant attention to this every time the clay is drawn up.

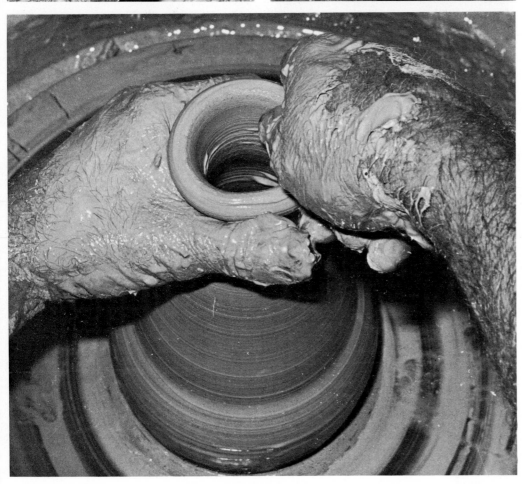

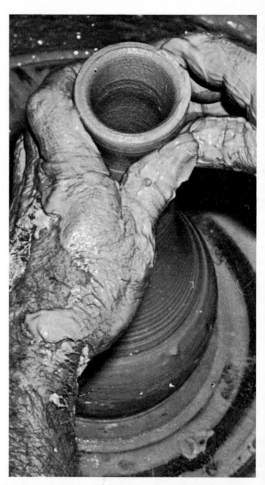

top left and right, bottom: True the top edge every time you draw up. As the neck becomes too narrow to get the fingers inside, work by applying pressure from points evenly spaced. The fingers lift at the same time pressing inwards.

top left: Pressure is kept even to the last moment. Gradually press in a little each time. The clay has been lifted many more times than illustrated here. Keep truing the top edge, otherwise it will be necessary to keep cutting pieces off the top and of course every time this happens the neck is just that much shorter.

top right: The base is cleaned up before the shape is cut off the wheel.

bottom: Cross sections showing the progress of the bottle.

throwing a narrow necked bowl

The top of this bowl will be brought into a small diameter. Centring, opening out and drawing into a cone are done exactly the same as in the making of a cylinder.

top left: Preliminary stages are as given for a cylinder. The fingers of the left hand are at the bottom of the cylinder. The index finger of the right hand braced by the thumb draws the clay up, working the clay into a bowl shape.

top right: The top is kept small, and the fingers stop their movement one inch to one-and-a-half inches from the top, steadying the bowl.

bottom: Pressure is applied with three fingers of the left hand inside the bowl mouth, the little finger and the thumb on the outside. The right hand is held as shown, with the fingers pushing inwards towards the centre of the wheel The pressure on the left little finger and thumb is inwards, drawing the neck inwards and making the top narrower. Have a healthy roll of clay left at this mouth to do any shaping of a rim or neck.

top left: Remove the excess clay at the point where the clay meets the wheel. The left hand is used to brace. The forefinger of the left hand gives support to the finger of the right hand as it removes the clay. Then shape the side. This could be your last chance to remove any water from the inside as the neck may be too small after the next movement.

top right: Widening out the belly of the bowl still further, using the hands in a similar manner until the shape is as desired.

bottom: The neck is now curved in and the edge is smoothed out by the same movement as previously described. Curve the neck by curving the fingers of the left hand over the thumb. Make the top edge run smoothly with the forefinger and thumb grip of the left hand. Steady the top of the rim with the middle finger of the right hand, assisted by the second smallest finger touching the outside.

See following five pictures for cut-away view of narrow top process.

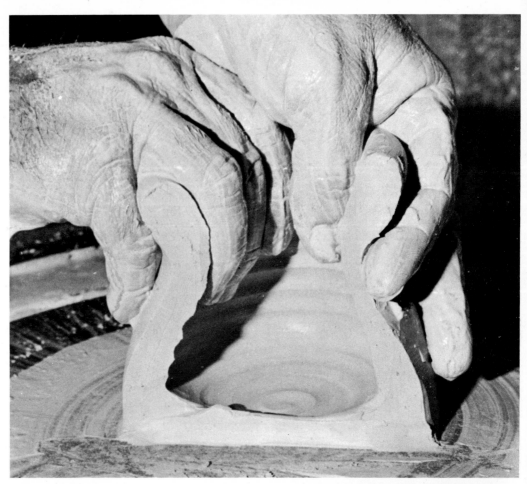

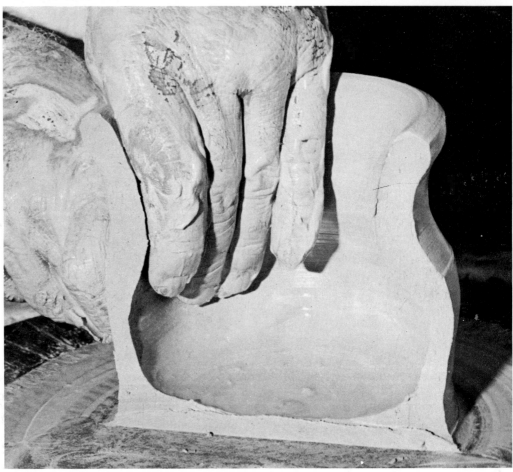

78

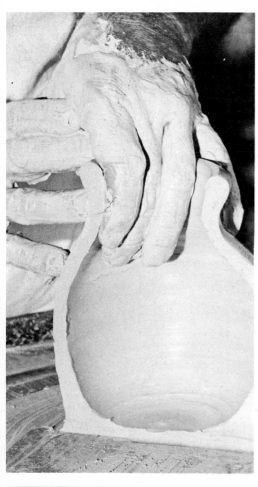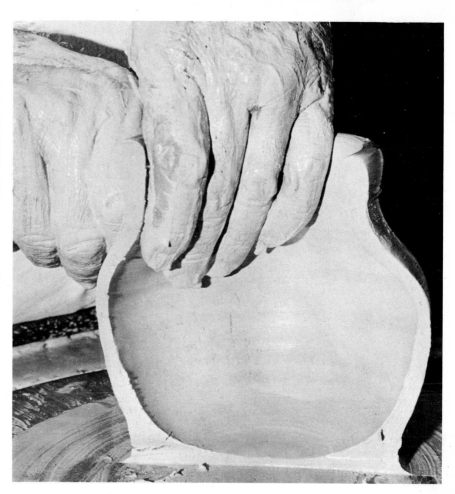

throwing a stopper for a bottle

Bottle tops can be made in many ways. You can make it as a cork-like shape, as described here, or as a cup shape which fits over the neck of the bottle.

top left: Centre the ball of clay.

top right, bottom left: The thumbs are pushed into the ball and a fine walled cylinder is drawn up.

bottom right: Narrow the cylinder about half way up its height to slightly less than the inside diameter of the neck of the bottle, and turn over the wall of the cylinder to close the neck of the stopper.

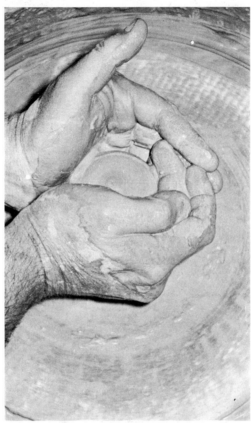

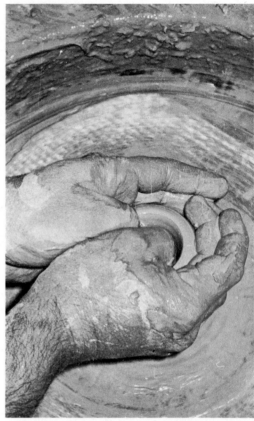

top, bottom: Check the diameter of the stopper with calipers and cut it from the wheel with a twisted wire. Allow for the thickness of glaze when measuring diameters.

81

A lidded vessel applied with an
iron glaze, then poured with a
matte talc glaze, and further
coloured by spraying with oxides.

The colours of this coffee pot have been created by using an iron glaze, wax resist brushwork followed by a hardwood ash glaze.

throwing a spout for a pot

Teapots, coffee pots, wine jugs and similar pots will need a spout.

top left: Centre a ball of clay and draw up a cone as thinly as possible to form a fine spout.

top right: Scribe a line around the base of the thrown cone and draw the wire around the line to cut off the spout.

bottom: Remove from the wheel, another cut at an acute angle will be needed to fit the base of the spout to the body of the pot.

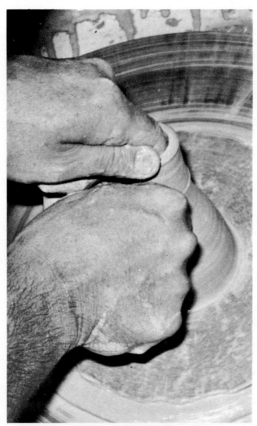

throwing a spout for a pot

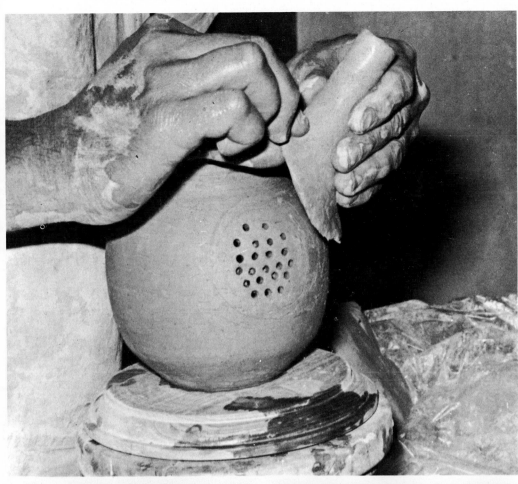

top: The body of the bowl (a teapot in this instance) is perforated with holes to act as a strainer, and the base of the spout is pulled slightly outwards to give it a flange easily pressed onto the bowl.

bottom left: Slurry is rubbed on to the surface to be adhered to the bowl of the teapot.

bottom right: The flange of the spout is pressed down onto the bowl. Cut the end of the spout at an angle horizontal with the ground plane, and at a level above that of the liquid to be held in the pot. Coffee pots and wine jugs usually dispense with the strainer and have only an open hole to the spout.

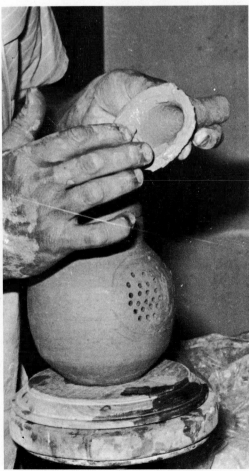

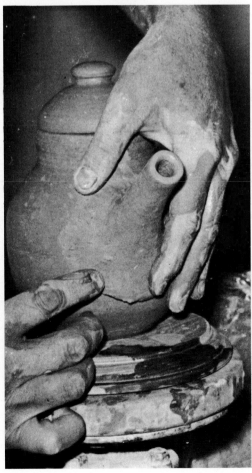

This bottle and corked jar have
been finished with a dolomite
glaze and sprayed with rutile
mineral sand.

A dolomite glaze and a glossy iron glaze with Ilmenite and rutile mineral beach sands were applied to this large plate.

throwing off a mound

A ball or mound of clay is placed on the potter's wheel. The whole may be centred, or just the portion which is to be shaped.

top: A small mound of clay is centred.

opposite bottom, top, bottom left:
A bowl is thrown. It is opened out
to the desired shape. The main
difficulty in this type of throwing
is to cut the piece cleanly off the
mound. Care should be taken to
recess or scribe the base of the
piece, so that the cutting wire can
be easily used to separate the
piece from the ware.

bottom right: A small pot made in
the same manner being cut from
a mound.

89

This wine jug has a zircon/
felspathic glaze over an iron
glaze.

The potter has applied a felspathic glaze over an iron glaze with a wax resist decoration on this bowl. Zircon, rutile, copper and cobalt oxides were also used.

throwing tiles for a wall

Throwing on a potters wheel can produce many other things than functional household ware.

Here is a decorative wall for a large office building. In this instance only the tile is the potter's creation. The colour and arrangement were the architect's conception. The tile is thrown in well grogged clay.

top: The clay is thrown, and leaving a small mound in the centre, a rim is pushed out.

centre: The rim is thinned and turned inwards.

bottom: It is then curled over and joined to the base.

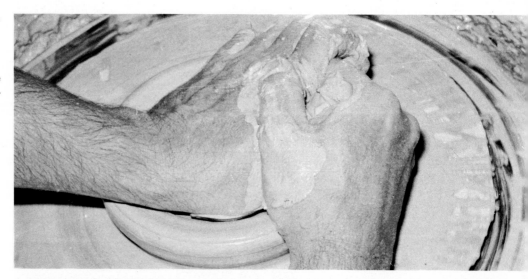

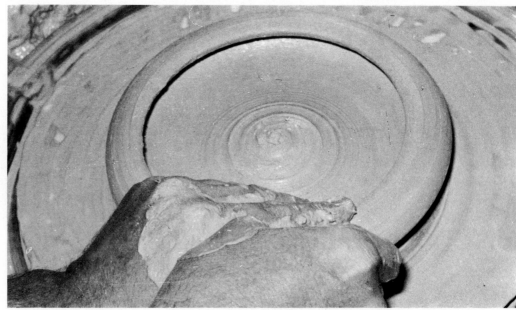

top, centre: The centre is opened out, and as it is thinned it is pulled into a dome.

bottom: The top is then sealed.

Various oxides and wax resist decoration were used between a hardwood ash and iron glazes to produce the effects on this plate.

This corked jar is an example of dolomite glaze on iron glaze.

top: The sides are squared by pushing them into shape with a steel tool. The dome is shown here as convex, others were concave.

bottom: Here are the two stages of the firing sequence. On the left is the tile after being in the biscuit kiln, it is then glazed, coloured and the trough filled with broken coloured glass. On the right is the tile after the glaze firing. After firing in the stoneware glaze kiln, the shrinkage can be observed, the colour is apparent, and the glass has melted to form a thick band of coloured glaze.

joining pieces on a wheel

Any number of pieces thrown on the wheel may be joined together. The size of the kiln available is the only restriction. Two pieces will give a vase or bottle shape as big as most studio kilns will take. The top half is thrown first and is left heavy. It is put aside to stiffen slightly.

right: The lower half is then thrown to its finished thickness. The top of the lower half, where the two pieces will be joined, is grooved or flanged to receive the top half. The lower half is then allowed to stiffen. Its top edge may be covered with a strip of plastic to keep it in good condition for joining.

joining pieces on a wheel

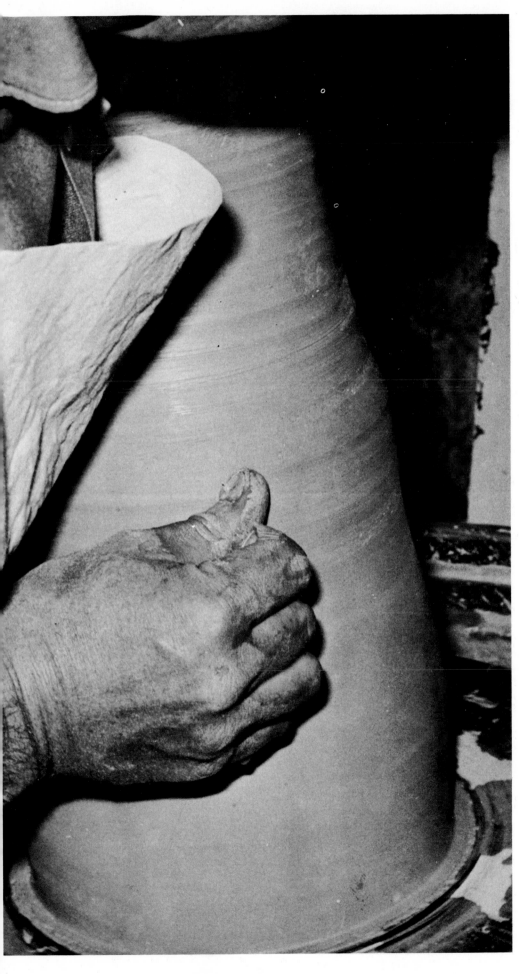

left: When it is stiff enough to support the top half, some slurry is applied to both surfaces so they may be joined. The top half is centred onto the flange and is welded onto the bottom. The thick bottom of the first thrown half, which is now the top, can be thinned and drawn up to form the neck of a bottle or the top of a vase or whatever design is desired.

pulling a handle

The best clay for pulling a handle is clay which has been maturing for some time. In this case, if the clay has been pugged or wedged previously, do not wedge or knead it again.

top: Form the clay into a cone-like shape. Then holding the widest section in one hand, pull it with the other using ample slurry as lubrication.

bottom: Decide on the length and width of the handle, and do not attempt to draw it any longer than desired, as this is just a waste of time, of no help in the design, and perhaps disastrous to the handle. Encircle the clay with the fingers to make a round handle.

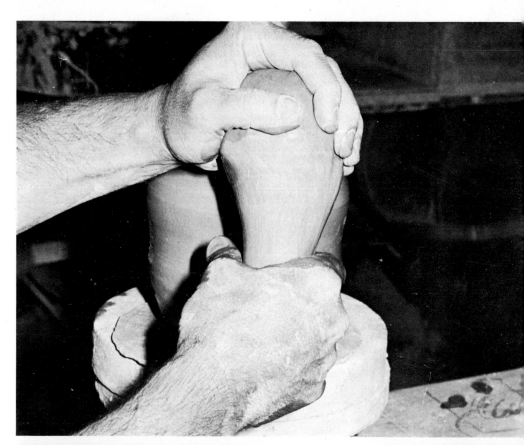

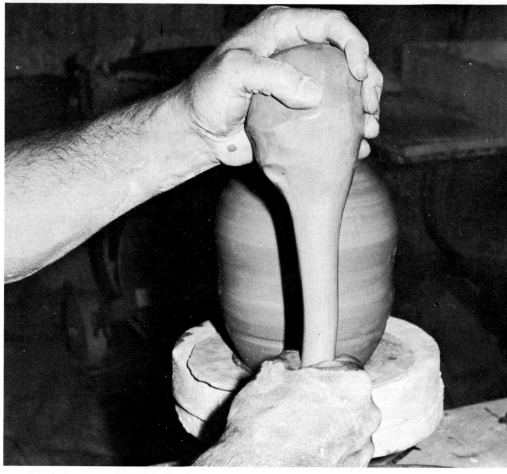

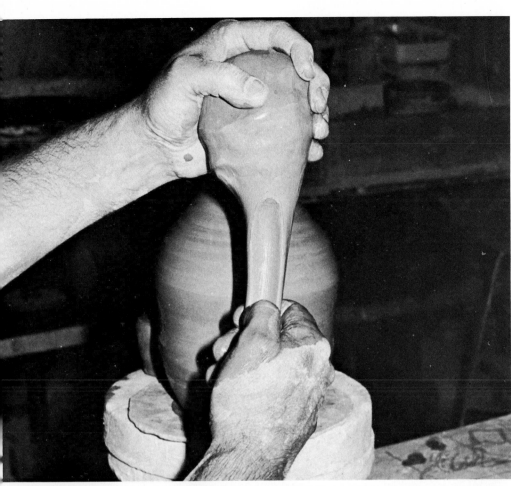

top: Use the thumb to flatten the clay for a wider, flatter handle. Only practise will give a fine rhythmic handle.

bottom: Allow the clay to stiffen for a little while.

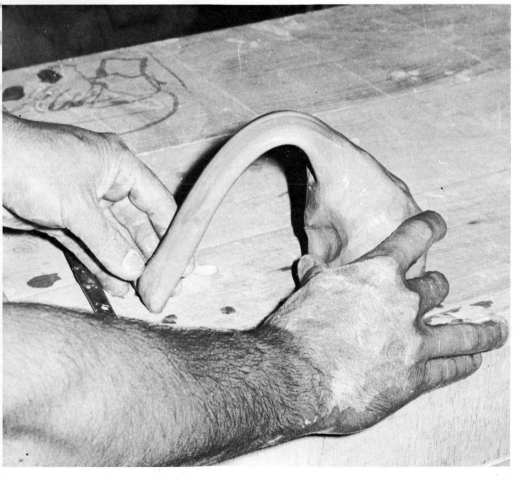

101

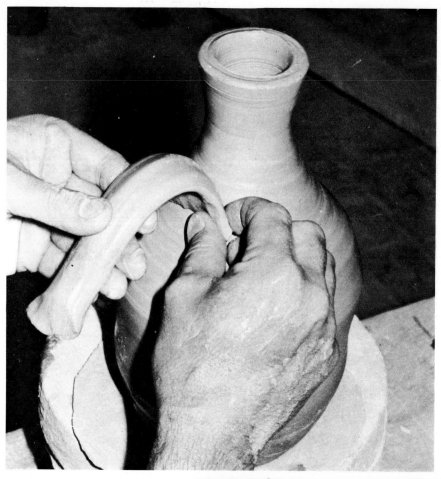

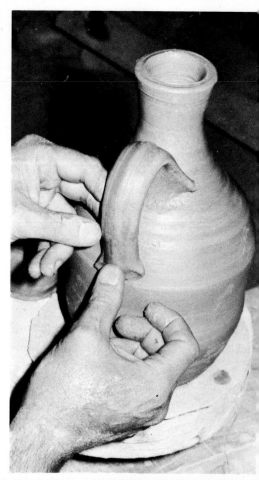

top left: Cut the handle to the desired length and attach the top of the handle to the form. If both bodies are plastic, no slurry will be needed. If drying has commenced on the main form, score the form and use slurry to assist in adherence.

top right: Press the handle onto the form, firmly enough to exclude all air and fix it on but not so hard as to push the main form out of shape.

bottom: If desired, little sausages of clay can be put into the crevices formed between the handle and the body for better unity.

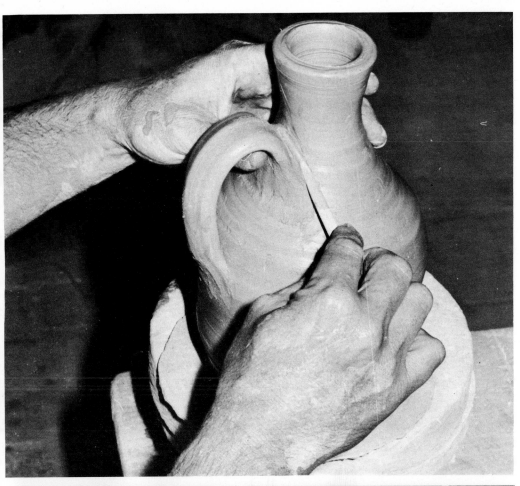

further useful throwing hints

top: The potter, when working on the wheel, looks down on to the piece being made. A mirror placed in a convenient position also allows the profile of the ware to be seen.

bottom: The mirror is also an asset when doing repetitive pieces.

opposite—
top left and right: Should cracking occur on a lid and it usually happens at the knob, this can be avoided by throwing the knob hollow.

bottom left and right: An expert potter can pick up a flat bowl by sliding his fingers under it, lifting, and placing it on a bat. This requires considerable skill to avoid distortion.

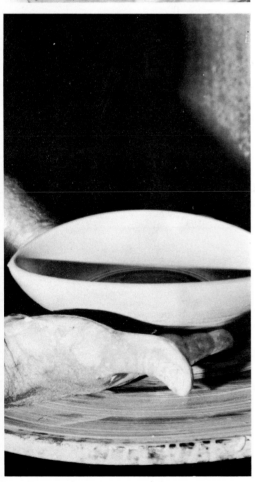

a cylinder becomes a jug

Throw a cylinder as described. A spout is then worked into the cylinder. One way of doing this is shown here.

top left: The index finger of the left hand supports under the spout. The thumb is placed at the side of the spout, whilst the wet right forefinger forms the spout.

bottom left: The hands are then changed over so that the same process is repeated, but with the opposite hands.

right: A handle is then pulled and attached to the form.

opposite: The jug is now finished.

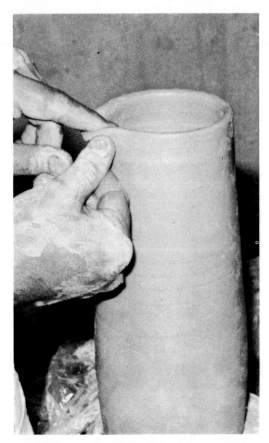

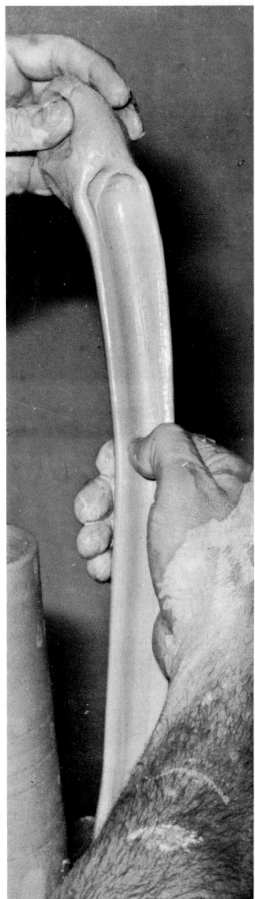

handbuilding

pinching a pot

During the making of this little pot, the hands should be kept clean and slightly moist. Dry hands, especially with dry clay on them, absorb the moisture from the clay causing it to crack.

top: Take a small ball of clay which will easily fit into the palm of the left hand, and a piece of paper about two inches in diameter. Slightly cone the ball of clay and flatten one end making sure the surface is smooth and without any flaws.

centre: Holding the clay in the left hand, press the right thumb into the flat end of the ball of clay. Turn it continually in the left hand. Do this until the bottom is almost the correct thickness and the ball is opened out sufficiently to allow for freedom for the thumb and fingers.

bottom: Place the little bowl on the piece of paper, gently flattening the base on it. The piece of paper will act as a bat allowing the clay to be freely rotated on the table whilst thinning the wall. Concentrate working round the foot of the pot keeping the rim thicker and rounded, making sure that no cracks appear. If they do, rub them out with a slightly moistened finger.

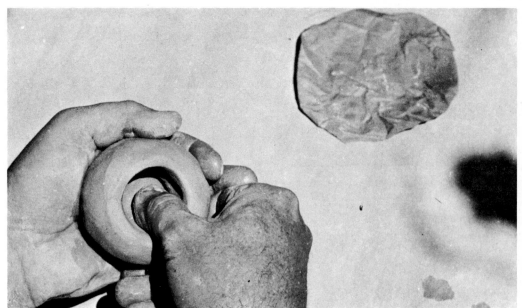

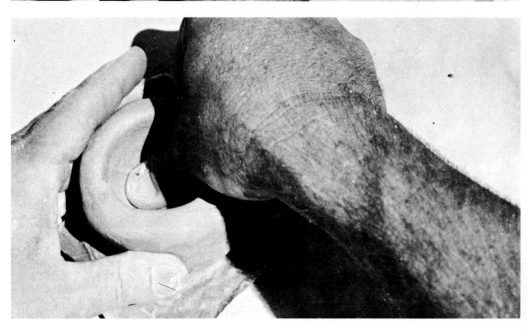

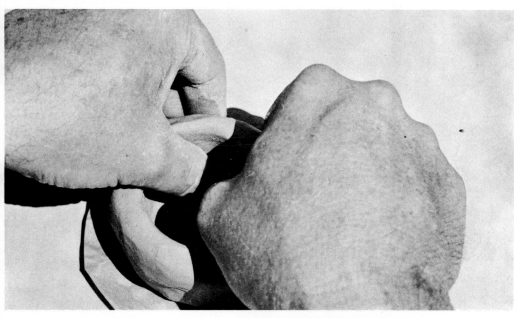

top: As the pot is opened out, two hands may be used, continually pinching the walls thinner and causing them to rise higher and higher whilst at the same time rotating the pot so that attention is given to every section of the wall. The rim is thinned last, and trimmed if desired.

centre: This process is continued until the wall is tidied. Throughout making, the pot may be picked up and rotated in the left hand if this will allow easier access to the walls and the base.

bottom: The pot is now finished. The Japanese made tea ceremony bowls in this way. This method can be used to make any open vessels. The size depends on the capabilities of the potter. A bowl made in this way acts as an excellent base upon which to build a coil piece.

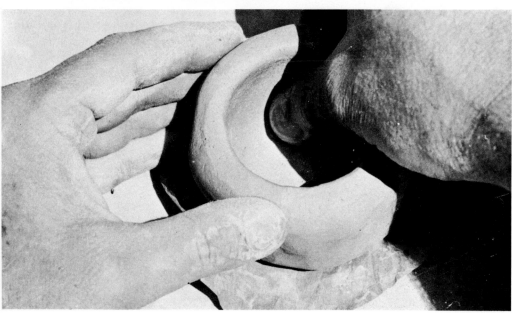

coiling on a pinched pot base

A pinch pot made as previously described makes an excellent base to build upon with coils.

top: Roll the clay horizontally with fingers spread apart, rotating the clay to its full diameter.

centre: The clay can be rolled vertically, but this requires more skill.

bottom: Join the rolled coils to the top edge of a pinch pot with a downward pressure of the thumb. The wrist is then rotated to allow the forefinger to press down and inwards on the outside. Further height can be quickly gained to make tall objects, although some time may have to be allowed at stages, for the walls to stiffen to support the extra weight.

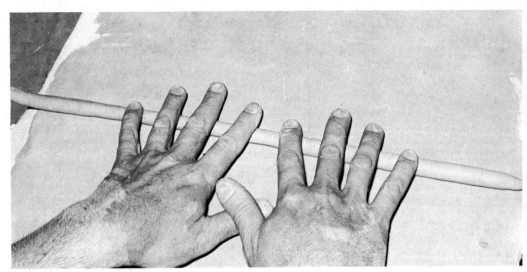

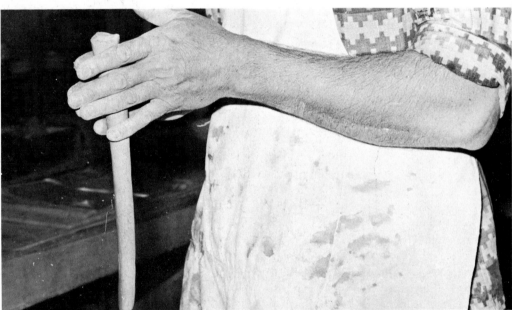

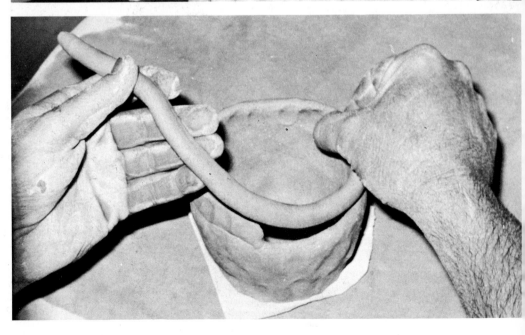

top left: A large lamp base made using this method, then beaten into planes, with some rolls of clay added to give the decorative shape on its upper half.

top right: After glaze firing — the finished base.

bottom: A profile is sometimes used when a specific shape is required. The piece is rotated on the wheel and the profile can be used like a cutting edge.

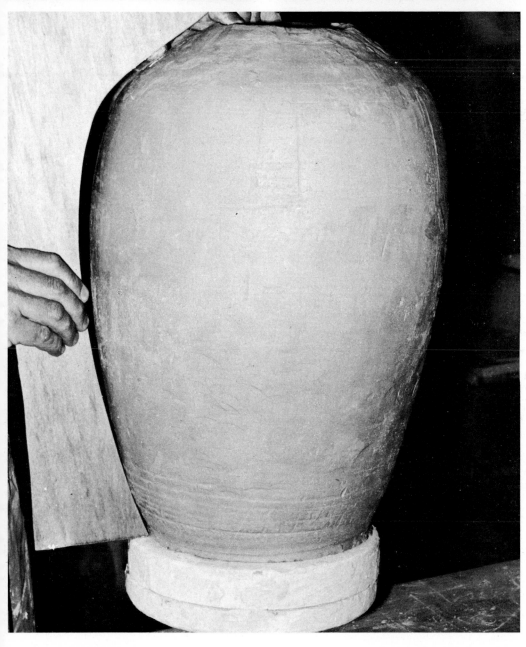

draping a shape

top: A clay form is made on whicn to drape a slab of clay. It is supported off the bat to leave room for trimming. Cheese-cloth is wrapped around the form to prevent the clay sticking.

bottom: A slab of clay is cut and laid over the form.

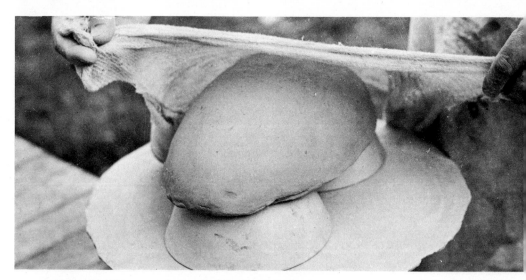

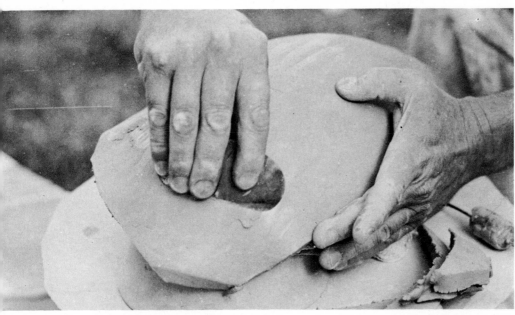

top: With a damp, flexible tool the clay is persuasively shaped to assume the contour of the form. Excess clay is removed from the rim as the process continues.

centre: The rim is then trimmed.

bottom: Three feet can be modelled and placed on the shape to see how they will look. A flat bat placed upon them will show if they are going to support the shape evenly.

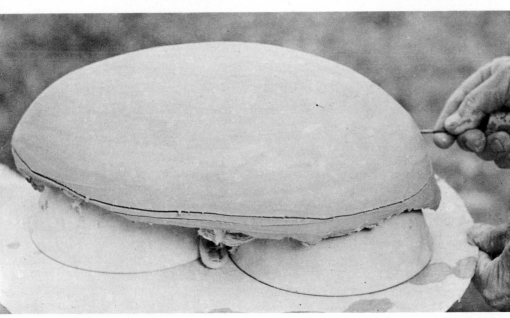

top: Mark the position of the feet.
Then score the feet and the surface
to which they will be adhered.
Thick slip is used to join them
firmly to the shape.

bottom: A surface pattern may be
added.

116

top: The bowl is removed from the mould form as soon as possible after it stiffens. If it is left too long it will shrink onto the mould and crack. The rim can be made level by rubbing it on an even wet coarse surface.

bottom: A drape shape.

slab building a free form shape

top: Using heavily grogged plastic clay, cut two slabs of about the same size. Then cut a narrower slab for the base. It must be the same length as the bottom of the sides. Put slurry on the portion to be joined.

bottom: Firmly pinch the base of the sides on to the base slab. The two sides are then pinched together in the same manner.

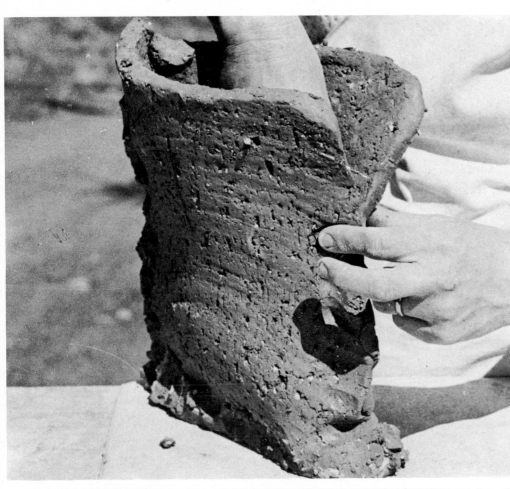

top: The shape is allowed to suggest its own form, and interesting bulks or rhythms are emphasised. For further or higher sides, a support would be required.

bottom: The finished form.

free form shapes

top: Heavily grogged clay is shaped into free forms to form a decorative mural. These shapes could equally well be used for dry arrangements, or a fountain in large forms.

bottom: The shapes suggest their overall arrangement. This design could be said to 'just happen'. To a degree it does because the potter allows the clay to freely suggest the form that results.

opposite—
top: The arrangement suggests a decorative mural. Selection is still required to choose the size of the pieces of clay and the combination of the forms.

bottom: Glaze is applied to the almost completed panel.

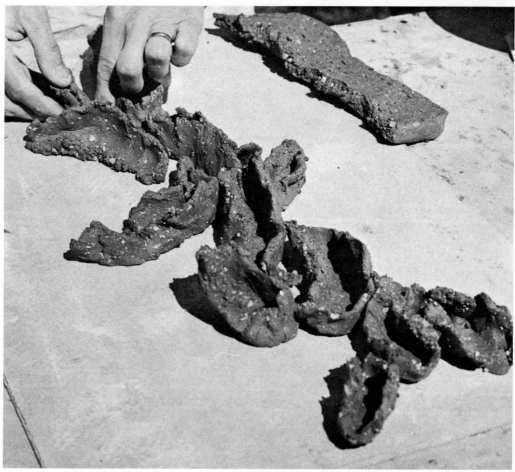

decorative panels

top left: A freeform panel, made by draping as described in the previous section.

top right: Another such panel, mounted on wood.

bottom: Circles of clay have been squared, and glued together to form a wall panel.

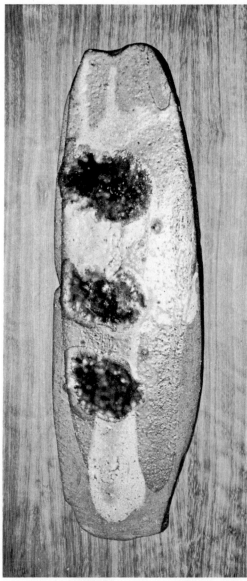

stoneware tiles

Stoneware tiles have a distinctive character. They look hard and strong — and they are. But the glaze can be soft, deep and lustrous. The restrained colour of stoneware glaze makes this type of tile harmonious with any modern interior decoration.

A table tiled with stoneware tiles is a simple but impressive project. Ample grog should be used in tile clay, up to thirty per cent may be used. Allowance should be made for shrinkage, so that a tile measuring six inches by six inches will probably be made six-and-three-quarter inches by six-and-three-quarter inches. Only a shrinkage test will give this, if it is important. In any case, it is wise to have the table made after the tiles are made, then you can be sure of accurate fitting. Here is a method of making tiles using a simple mould. Make the clay shape in its preshrunk size with its bottom upwards. Then make a plaster mould of it. The tools required will be a length of canvas or some similar material, cutting wire, a needle, a large palette knife, two strips of wood about half an inch thick, a rubber mallet, some cheesecloth or muslin, a paint scraper, a small steel straight edge, a bag of silica and a pattern of the tile in its preshrunk size, which of course will be the same size as the tile shape in the plaster mould. A number of pieces of asbestos cement wall board slightly larger than the tile size will be required to dry the tiles between.

top left and right: Prepare the clay, well grogged and fairly stiff. Wedge and thump it into a suitable shape. Place a piece of canvas on the table to stop the clay from sticking. Place two half inch wooden strips each side of the clay and guide the cutting wire by these strips as you pull it through the clay to give an even slab.

bottom: Prepare the mould, making sure it is clean. Shake a cotton bag of silica over it to deposit a thin film of dust. The dust will help to prevent the clay sticking to the mould.

top: Place the tile pattern on the clay. Keeping the needle vertical, cut around the pattern, remove any 'rags' which might be around the edge.

centre left: Carefully lift the clay slab square into the mould. Press it in firmly with the ball of the hand to seat it fully.

centre right: Cover the whole with a piece of muslin. Use a rubber mallet to flatten the clay further. Work from the centre outwards. Avoid striking the edges of the mould.

bottom left and right: Remove the muslin. Place the steel rule at the centre of the mould. Draw it firmly towards the body, removing any excess clay from the top. Turn the mould around and repeat on the other half. Repeat until the surface is flat.

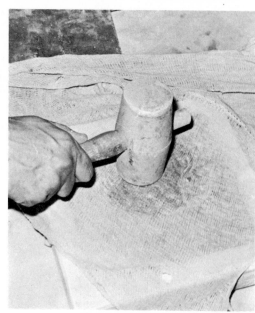

124

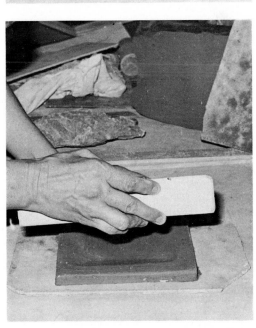

top left: Any small marks can be removed with a paint scraper. In all these operations be careful not to chip the edges of the mould. Place the mould aside for the clay to stiffen.

top right, centre left: Leave aside to set and stiffen. You will see that the clay pulls away from the sides of the mould. Loosen the tile with a sharp downward tap on the side of the mould from which clay is pulling away. Place the square of asbestos cement over the mould and turn them over, keeping them firmly together.

centre right, bottom: Remove the mould. Sandwich the clay tile between two pieces of asbestos cement to dry. You can place tiles four high between alternating squares of asbestos cement. Do not put them higher than this because the weight will crack the bottom tile. Turn the tiles upside down several times while they are drying, but keep them between the asbestos cement because this assures even drying on both sides of the tile and prevents warping. When the tile is dry it can be sandpapered along the edges and fired.

125

textured tiles

The making of tiles presents many possibilities of design to the potter. On flat tiles interesting effects can be created with glaze, using the glaze to convey the design. Again the potter may be preoccupied with textures and surface contrasts, or three dimensional concepts. Tiles can be used for mass effect or spot decoration. Their surface may be smooth for functional purposes, such as a table top. They may be made in the deepest of relief for decorative purposes.

Tiles with textural surfaces are easy to make and can be used in many ways. Any form can be impressed into the clay to create a design on the tile.

top: Cut a well-grogged piece of clay about half an inch thick. Take a length of muslin and cover the clay. In this illustration an unusual weathered piece of limestone is used to impress a pattern on the clay with a rolling action.

centre: When the cloth is removed, the pattern is revealed.

bottom: A paint scraper can also be used to make a pattern.

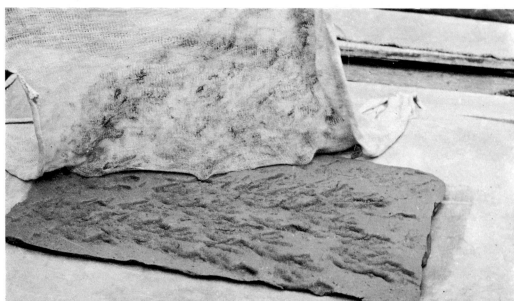

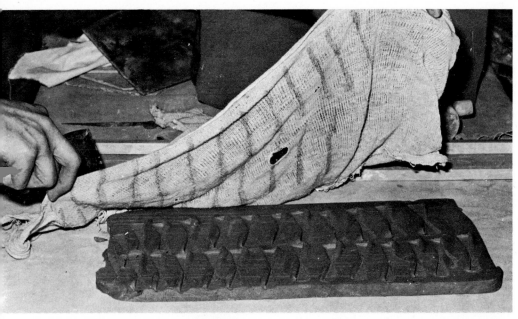

top: The unusual design made by the use of the paint scraper.

centre: Cut the tiles into their planned sizes and place them between asbestos cement sheets to dry.

bottom: Tiles of different designs can be placed together for the top of a coffee table.

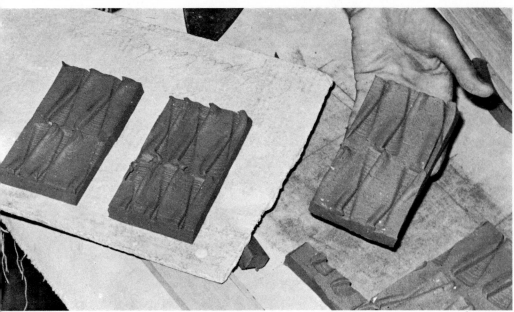

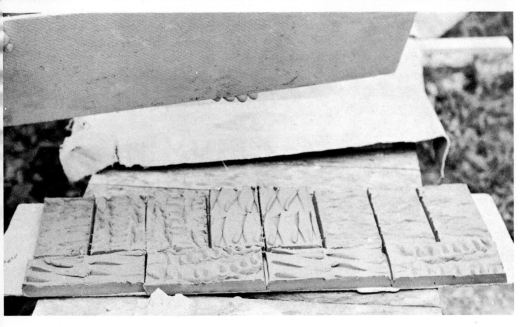

handbuilding combined with throwing
a lamp base

Many ways of combining various means of making will become apparent with practice. A simple cylinder can be used as it is made, shaped as shown, beaten into oval or squared shapes, or combined with other forms.

top: Wrap a cardboard cylinder in newspaper. Keep one end of the newspaper flush with an end of the cylinder.

centre: Roll a slab of clay onto the cylinder. Keep one edge of the clay slab flush with an edge of the cylinder.

bottom left: Pinch in the sides of the slab and join them.

bottom right: Cut off the excess clay. Smooth the join with a flexible kidney rubber.

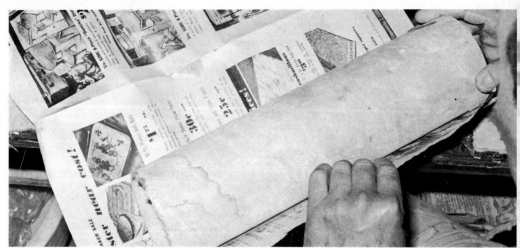

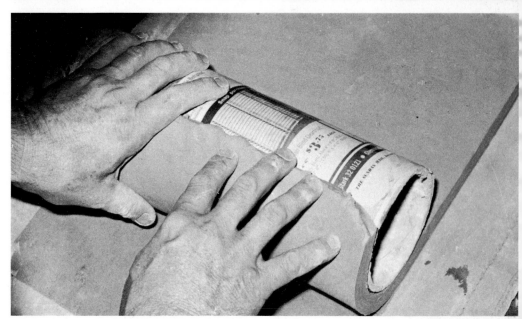

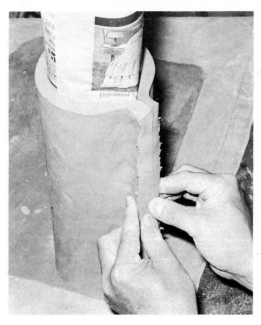

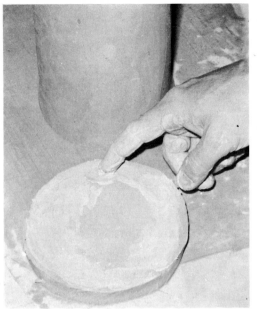

top left: Place the cylinder on another slab of clay. Cut a circle slightly larger than the base diameter of the cylinder. This circle will form the base.

top right: Smear the base with slurry where the cylinder will join it.

bottom: Place the cylinder on the base. Draw the excess clay upwards to weld the two pieces together.

top left: Grasp the cardboard cylinder and draw it up through the paper. Then remove the paper from inside the clay cylinder.

top right: Weld the joins inside the cylinder with thin sausages of clay. Even up the thickness of the clay.

bottom left: Throw a circlet of clay slightly larger than the diameter of the cylinder. Place the cylinder within it.

bottom right: Make sure the cylinder is truly centred, then push the circlet of clay into the cylinder to hold it firmly.

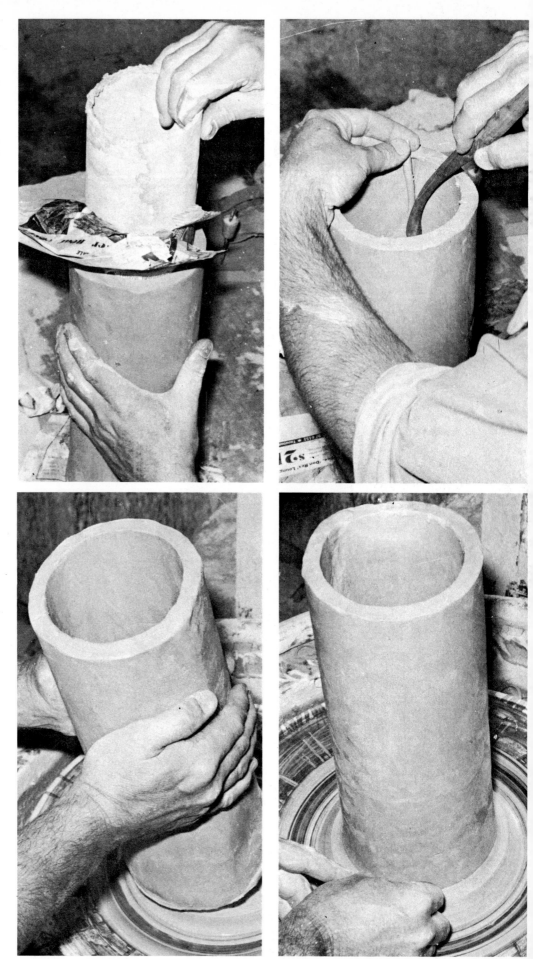

top left: This shape is now ready to make into a bottle or lamp base. Draw it upwards and make it run true.

top right: Steady the rim and draw it inwards.

bottom: The shape is now suitable for a lamp base. It can be used as it is or shaped further.

coiling on a thrown base

top: First throw the base shape. In this illustration the base shape is a thrown bowl. You may have to allow some time for the base shape to stiffen enough to support extra weight. Next join a coil to the base shape using the normal method for coil building.

bottom: Draw up the clay as in normal throwing.

132

left: Continue drawing up the clay until you have reached the height and shape you want. In this illustration, the coil has been made into a bottle neck.

133

Moulds have probably been used for making pottery since the earliest times. Ancient potters making repetitive shapes such as plates or bowls undoubtedly used cane baskets as moulds which allowed for repetition of the same shape with minimum effort. Moulds are widely used all over the world for pottery production. In the west, they are mainly used for mass commercial production. In Asia, many highly prized shapes are moulded, such as rectangular bottles and bonsai and ikebana containers.

Should the potter desire to make shapes to a particular model and to repeat these forms, he uses a mould. (See illustrations on making a mould for a simple bowl for step by step instructions.) The artist-potter usually makes such moulds of soft biscuited clay or plaster of Paris. Both these raw materials give the necessary absorbency which brings about the stiffening of the clay. Most potters use plaster of Paris to make their moulds because it is cheap and easy to use, though many choose the finer dental plaster, which sets quickly and is of a fine grain which causes its surface to remain smooth as it wears. Models can be made from any modelling material, but of course clay will be the easiest and most available medium.

Any article can be cast. However, if the model has returns (sections from which the clay form cannot be withdrawn) multi-piece moulds must be made. When necessary, soft soap is the usual medium used to coat the surface of the model to prevent the plaster sticking.

The form can be made in the mould using either plastic or liquid clay. Plastic clay is usually cut into slabs and pressed into the mould by hand. Other similar processes on the wheel will be described. Moulding with liquid clay is known as slip casting.

4

moulds

slip casting

Slip casting is another method of making repeated shapes. The method depends on having an open, fairly non-plastic clay body which can be made into a liquid slip with a minimum quantity of water to enable clay forms to be made without undue shrinkage and consequent cracking.

The clay is *deflocculated* – that is turned into a liquid slip (known as casting slip) by the use of chemicals such as sodium silicate and/or soda-ash, with a period of mixing. This allows twenty to forty per cent water (by weight) to be used, instead of the greater quantity which would be necessary without the use of deflocculents. The resulting liquid clay is poured into plaster moulds and allowed to stand until it is the correct thickness for the article being made. This is accomplished by the water in the clay passing from the open clay body into the walls of the absorbent mould. As the water is gradually removed from the bulk of liquid clay within the mould, the clay begins to solidify from its outside edge. When this hardening reaches the required thickness the remaining liquid clay within the mould is poured out leaving the clay form. Any waste portion is then trimmed. As the clay dries further, it parts from the mould, and is then usually firm enough to be removed. It can then be turned and have attachments added. For example, handles of cups or jugs can be added at this stage.

A casting slip may prove difficult for a small potter to make. The first problem is finding clays of a suitable nature. It may be necessary to buy at least a kaolin from a mineral supplier. If a clay is used that is plastic or greasy, it will soon form a film on the mould surface. This will restrain the water from being absorbed. The second problem is the obstinate refusal of some clays to be satisfactorily deflocculated.

Casting slip is improved in quality the longer it is mixed and the longer it is kept before using. Soft water should be used.

As the factors are variable, luck plays a great part in the time necessary to find a suitable casting recipe. You may find a clay which will deflocculate (turn into a liquid slip) with the correct proportions of water and deflocculent.

The percentage of water to dry materials is approximately twenty to forty per cent in weight. Rain or demineralized water is preferable to tap water. Usually if the clay or clays will deflocculate easily, the body still has to be balanced to prevent excessive shrinkage, warping or other faults. This balance is achieved with the addition of silica, kaolin and feldspar as previously described in the chapter on clay. Sodium silicate, soda-ash or water softeners like Calgon may be used on their own or together to deflocculate clay. The proportion of the deflocculent is usually up to .3 per cent of the dry clay weight.

As a very rough test put ten parts of the chosen clay or clays into four parts of water. Slowly add sodium silicate and observe the results. If the clay deflocculates or shows signs of deflocculating, further tests can be commenced. Measure similar small quantities of water and add proportions of various deflocculents to them. Add the clay and mix well. The results will give further indications of the direction to follow.

Slip making is mainly a matter of experiment, and from here the quantities will resolve themselves. The quantities of flux and fillers are added to perform their work in the body. Silica and feldspar are the main ones used. Casting slip should be mixed as long as practicable and allowed to age. It will work better after ageing several days.

There is no reason for cast ware to be dull and unimaginative. The glaze treatment can be lively. Cast pieces can be shaped and joined into many forms. Imagination can take the dullness from casting by finding many combinations. Cast objects can be joined or shapes can be beaten with a paddle to give individuality in the design of repetitive pieces.

faults and their cure in slip casting

There are many common faults in slip casting. A fine plastic clay will present problems in deflocculating and casting.

Soluble salts in clay may cause the slip to become sludgy after being in the mould a short time, this is commonly called livering. The addition of .25 per cent to .5 per cent of barium carbonate will make these salts insoluble. If this does not work, reduce the soda ash content, if this is being used, and increase the sodium silicate. Check to see that no plaster of Paris from the moulds is in the slip.

Pouring the slip from too great a height, or only in one spot may cause faults. Pinholing can be caused by air trapped in the slip. This is due to the slip being too thick, or carelessly poured. Try pouring it back and forth between two containers or fine sieving.

If any air is trapped in the mould, it will prevent the slip casting at this point. Tilt the mould, or perhaps make a higher head on the mould. Half filling the mould with slip and shaking before filling will help.

Cracking can be caused by any number of reasons:- There could be too great a proportion of silicate of soda in the slip, or the mould may be too dry, or there could be too much water in the slip, or the mould may be incorrectly made so as to cause uneven drying.

Finally, three major faults to watch in making slips are:-
i. If the slip becomes hard, then it has a high silicate percentage.
ii. Should it be thick and soft, it has too much soda ash.
iii. A thick sludgy layer indicates livering.

Prior to pouring into the mould, the clay should be remixed then sieved to eliminate any lumps and gelled portions formed by standing. The slip is poured into the mould, preferably to one side, so that air bubbles can escape with the rise of the clay and the mould is then left to stand until the desired thickness of the article is reached. The mould may need topping up as water is absorbed. The mould if it is small enough can have some of the slip poured off; then it should be lightly shaken to get the slip moving so it will run cleanly and then, when emptied, the mould should be placed upside down on a slight angle and left to drain.

After draining, the mould is turned upright again. The excess clay is trimmed from the piece as soon as possible as it it easier to do this before the edges shrink and pull away from the mould. Remember the plaster mould is easily worn by hard edged tools and trimming should be done with care. Smooth any faults inside the piece whilst the mould still supports the shape.

As soon as the cast piece shrinks away from the mould it is ready to remove. With every casting additional water is absorbed into the mould thus slowing down the casting. A sharp downwards tap on the edge of the mould will loosen any obstinate piece. For some shapes a bat can be placed over the mouth of the mould and the piece turned onto it.

Finishing can now be done with the stiffened form.

making a mould for a simple bowl

top: A bowl is an easy project to begin with. Shape a solid ball of clay into the inverted bowl shape with a base as described under it. Allow for shrinkage. The outside diameter of the mould will be the same as that of the base. Make the base several inches high to give the linoleum or tar paper wall something firm to wrap around. Leave a step. This protects the edge of the bowl shape by placing it lower than the top surface of the mould. The step is a guide for trimming the rim with a wire tool. This is a simple one piece mould and there are no returns to prevent the finished article coming out of the mould as it shrinks when drying.

centre: Use tarred paper, linoleum or other material as a form to hold the plaster, wrap it well around the model, and tie it firmly. Take care not to damage the model. Build up clay around the base in case any plaster leaks through.

bottom: Sprinkle the plaster over the estimated quantity of water in some easily cleaned container, such as a plastic bucket. Continue sprinkling quickly until the plaster is level with the top of the water, so that it quickly wets. Do not touch the plaster until it is all damp. Plaster sets quickly. If any above the surface does not wet within a couple of seconds, gently sprinkle a few drops of water on the obstinate parts. This will prevent delay in mixing. If you are mixing a small quantity use a large spoon or paddle.

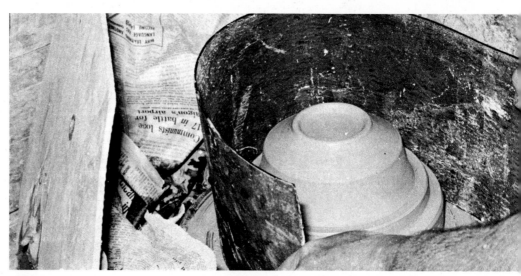

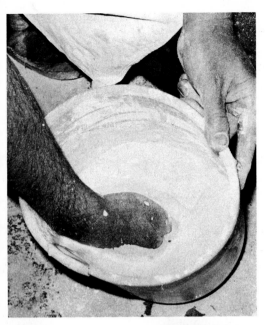 

top left: Most potters use their hand for mixing. Wear a plastic glove if your skin is sensitive. Hold your hand in the plaster. Move your fingers in such a way to rapidly push any air upwards to the surface of the plaster. Stir it, so that all lumps are broken up and the plaster is made into a smooth homogeneous mix.

top right: When the plaster is just stiff enough to retain the suggestion of a mark made on its surface with the finger, it is ready to pour.

centre: Pour the plaster smoothly on the side of the model, so that it rises around it expelling air. When the model is sufficiently covered, vibrate the table or wheel which it is on to cause any air to rise to the surface. If the model is solid and cannot be marked by touching, put your hand into the plaster and your fingers along any ridges to remove air bubbles.

bottom: Remove the supporting forms as soon as the plaster has set to a cheese-like consistency. Turn the semi-hard plaster and tidy up the mould. You will find the mould is easy to trim when the plaster is semi-hard. Fine work can be done later when the plaster is set hard. Use fine 'wet-and-dry' paper to remove any irregularities. Repair any minor faults. A little dry plaster placed in an air hole will wet and set. Round any edges on the outside which may be knocked and chipped when the mould is in use.

making multi-piece moulds

As pieces to be moulded become more complex in shape it will be apparent they cannot be formed in a simple one piece mould. It will be necessary to mould them in a multipiece mould of two or more pieces.

Salt and pepper shakers have this problem because the base of the mould must come away in the opposite direction to that part of the mould which forms the main shape. Make the mould in the same way as a bowl (shown on page 138). But in this case, the step is used as a registration or fitting guide for the base. After the plaster is poured, turned and set, remove the clay base to the point where the actual base of the salt and pepper shaker is. This is made concave to allow the cork to be below the line of the base.

Apply soft soap to the plaster where the next section will be poured, until water is repelled from its surface. Make sure there are no returns in the base which will prevent the next plaster piece being removed. Place a well greased tube where the hole of the salt and pepper will be. This will also act as the pouring hole for the slip clay. Wrap the mould and pour again. Trim the plaster as before. Remove the tube where the pouring hole will be.

When the plaster begins to feel warm and hard, have some boiling water on hand and pour this on the crack between the two pieces of the mould. If you are lucky, you will be able to pull the two pieces apart. If the pieces have a deep join, you may have to prise them apart by carefully tapping a wedge, such as a knife blade, into the crack. Then finish off the mould in the same manner.

The only difference in making a mould of free forms is that clay may have to surround the model to the parting line to make the form to contain the plaster.

Any shape which has to be repeated lends itself to being moulded. These include tiles, jewellery, bowls, mugs and so on. In some cases it is an advantage if uniformity is desired. In others, it results in loss of character. The potter must decide this question with a view to aesthetics as much as convenience.

Remember that plaster is a nuisance in clay, and may explode in the kiln. While making a mould, cover the wheel and surrounding areas with paper or plastic. Discard any used clay which you suspect of having plaster in it. You can use the plaster scraps as lime on the garden. Clean up very well. Do not allow any plaster to go down the sink. It will clog.

slip casting using a simple open mould

Before pouring the slip into the mould, remix and sieve the clay to eliminate any lumps or gellied portions formed by standing.

left: Pour the slip into the mould to one side so that air bubbles can escape as the clay rises. The clay will rise up higher than the mould without running over. Then leave the mould to stand until enough clay has hardened to give the required thickness of the article you want. You may have to top up the mould with slip as the water is removed.

right: Rotate the mould to bring the slip into solution.

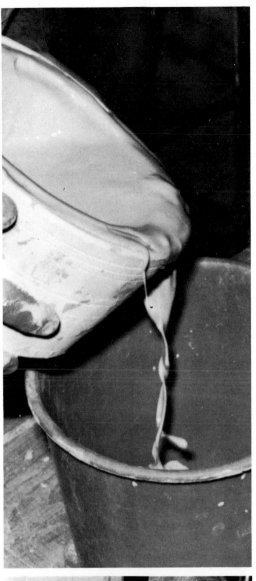

top left: Pour off the excess slip with a smooth action.

top right: Leave the mould to drain on a slight angle. After draining, turn the mould upright again.

bottom left: Trim off the excess clay from the rim of the bowl until it is level with the mould. Trimming should be done as soon as possible because it is easiest before the edges shrink and pull away from the mould. Trim with care because hard-edged tools can easily wear the plaster. Smooth any faults inside the bowl while the mould still supports the shape.

bottom right: As soon as the bowl shrinks and parts from the mould, place a bat over the mould and turn everything upside down. Lift off the mould to reveal the clay shape. If the clay form sticks, a downward blow on the side that shows signs of coming away from the mould will release the shape. Finish the piece in the usual way when the clay is stiff enough.

casting with a two piece mould

top left: Well mixed slip is poured into a two piece mould in the first stage of producing a pair of salt and pepper shakers.

top right: When the clay has stiffened to make a thick enough form, the mould is shaken to liquify the excess of clay slip. This is then poured out leaving the hollow shape.

bottom left: After further time for stiffening, the mould is tapped to loosen the piece which is then taken out.

bottom right: The turning wheel is used to remove the join mark of the mould, and to make a hole of the correct size to receive the cork.

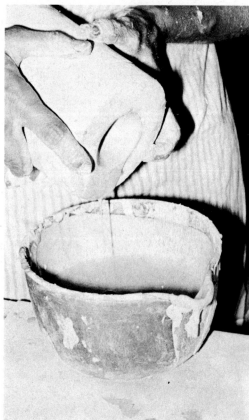

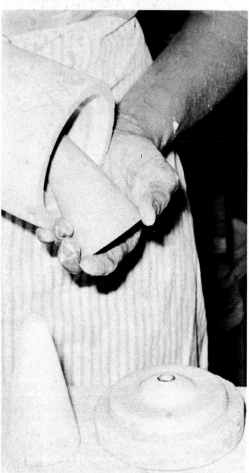

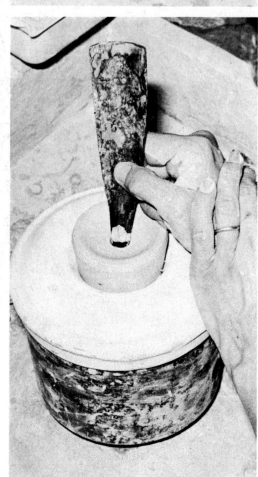

other examples of moulds

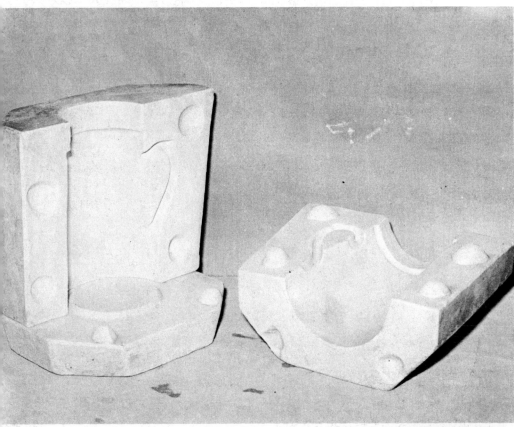

top: A three-piece mould for casting a tankard.

bottom left: Using a two piece mould to cast salt and pepper shakers.

bottom right: A shape which can be formed into a vase, coffee pot, or another form.

143

using a mould
to make a plate on the wheel

top: A plate mould is placed on a special head.

bottom, opposite top and bottom: Dust the mould lightly with silica in a cotton bag. Then place a pancake of clay on the mould and press it into shape with the fingers as the wheel revolves.

top: Then carefully remove any waste around the edge with a needle. Be careful not to mark the plaster mould.

bottom: Use a flexible tool to smooth the plate.

Opposite —
top left: The rim is rounded and the plate is ready to set aside for some time to stiffen. When the rim separates from the mould, the plate is ready to be removed. This is best accomplished by tapping the mould with a downward glancing blow until the plate is loosened. Then place a flat asbestos cement bat over its surface and turn the lot upside down. Then remove the mould. If the plate is still soft, repeat the process onto another bat, so that the large unsupported bottom will not sag. This is a comparatively simple process and allows the inexperienced potter to make a large shape with ease.

top right: A simple open mould may be used on a circlet of clay on the wheel.

bottom: The mould is tapped into the centre and the method described above can be used.

146

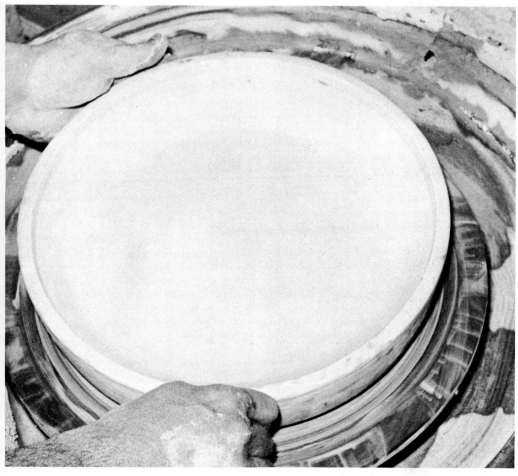

jiggering a bowl

A jigger or jolly wheel is a device for making repeated shapes. Moulds are made to fit a special wheel head. An arm with a profile of the inside of the shape is used to form the clay.

When making plates and other flat shapes the profile is often used to shape the base of the piece. The mould forms the inside of the plate.

top: Dust the mould lightly with silica. Place a perfectly smooth ball of clay within it.

bottom left: Using just enough slurry, the fingers open the ball of clay, keeping a fat wall near the top edge of the mould.

bottom right. Throw a splash of slurry into the bowl for lubrication. Draw down the profile to shape the inside of the bowl. As a slight excess of clay is used, some will have to be removed from the top edge of the mould during making. Clear clay from the profile if it builds up excessively.

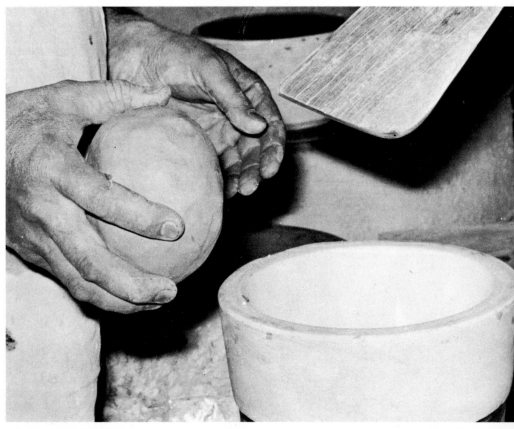

jiggering a bowl

top left: Round the inside of the rim with a finger.

top right: After a time, the drying form shrinks away from the mould. A sharp downward blow on the side where the clay has shrunk furthest from the mould will release the whole bowl.

bottom: The bowl can be taken out and allowed to stiffen further. Only the outer edge of the rim should need attention in turning. The mould is now ready to be used again.

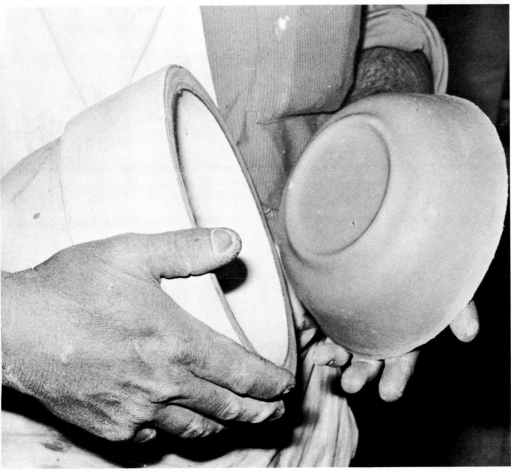

149

press moulding a handle

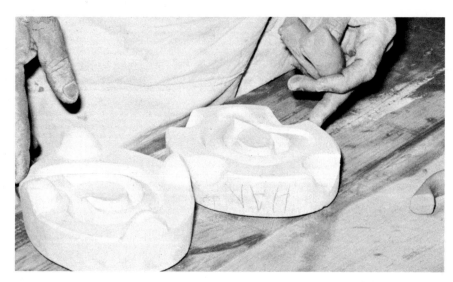

top left: A two piece press mould can be used to make a handle. The negative shape (in this case a handle) is surrounded by a trough into which the excess clay travels as the two pieces of the mould are pressed together.

top right: Place a roll of clay slightly larger than the finished size in the negative shape of the mould. Then press the two moulds together. Press on a firm table, preferably over a leg where no give is possible. The sharp edge left around the join line acts as a cutter to cut the waste almost through. It is important that the two mould pieces are exactly opposite one another during pressure so they are not damaged.

centre: After the first pressure the mould pieces may still not quite join together. Remove the waste clay from the trough and press again.

bottom: Clean the waste off again and a handle results. Many shapes are suitable to be made this way. But handles are the most common in this type of production.

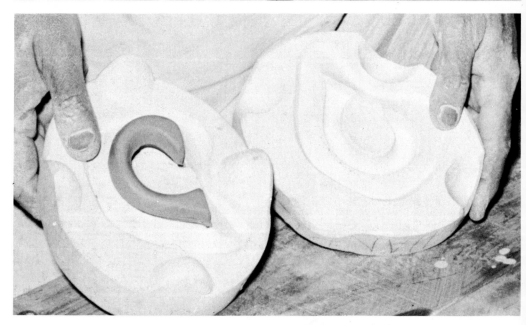

sprig moulding

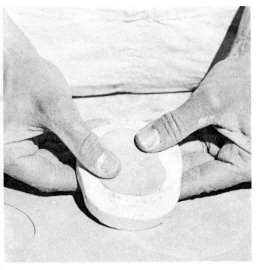

top left: Sprig moulding is done by pressing clay into a simple mould to form a shape which will be embossed onto the main body. Wedgwood ware is perhaps the major example of this. A model is made and plaster of Paris is poured over it to make a small mould. The mould is dusted and clay is forced into it, and then trimmed level with the mould.

top right: Remove the decoration, using another piece of clay or the damp blade of a palette knife.

centre left: Apply some slip to the back of the decoration.

centre right: Apply the decoration firmly to the surface of the vase and smooth the edges.

bottom: In the finished piece the decoration has changed a simple beaker into a souvenir piece.

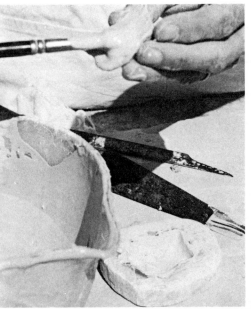

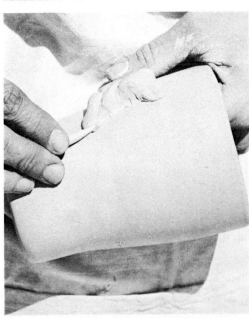

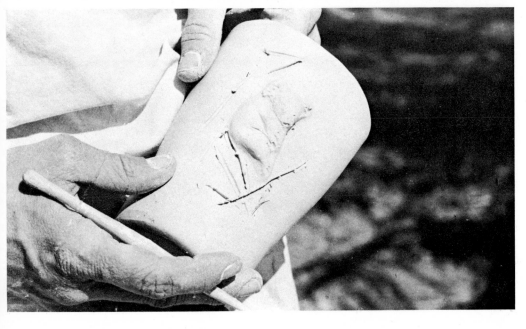

joining simple moulded pieces

There are numerous ways of joining pieces and decorating.

top: A simple method is shown here using two cast cups.

bottom: Apply slip to the surfaces to be joined which have first been turned true. Centre one piece on the wheel, then centre the other piece and join it on. Turn and sponge the join.

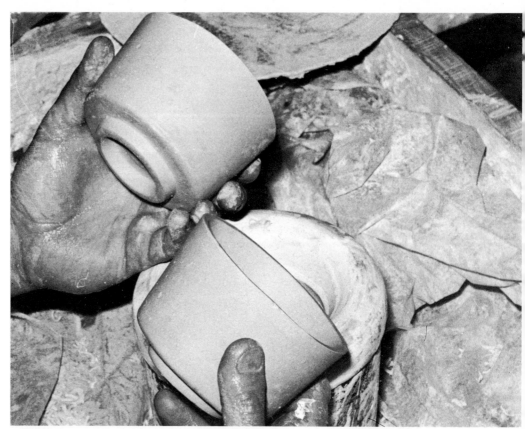

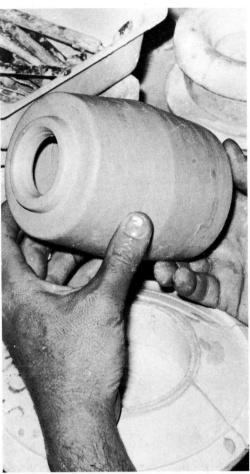

top left and right: Cut a hole through one end.

bottom left: Mix red oxide with some slip, then brush it on the shape.

bottom right: As the slip is fast drying, a design can be done in sgraffito almost immediately.

right, opposite top: The piece is later glazed in a transparent glaze. The glaze can be a matt or opaque, this allows the oxide to bleed through and give a more subtle effect.

opposite bottom: Slipcasting using imagination. This shows how three individual forms on the right of the picture can be joined to make a coffee pot.

5

design
and
decoration

design

Personal taste in design is something that grows. It is a gradually expanding knowledge passing from the obvious local conceptions to an understanding of historical work from primitive times until today. If this learning is done logically, a sound foundation will be built. By now, it should be obvious that the nature of the potter's working material has a great influence on the finished design of the piece. With soft clay, there will be many limitations in the height that can be thrown and in the amount of overhang on a bowl. Such clay will enable a weak potter to centre and throw quite a large platter. A strong clay may allow all types of shapes to be thrown. But, if the clay is heavy and stiff, it may restrict the size of the ware owing to the difficulty of centring.

Handbuilding is governed by the same rules. As the work takes longer, the clay has more time to stiffen and thus more complex shapes can be made. The clay should be well-grogged which will give it strength and enable it to dry without cracking. But theory is useless here. In the beginning, intuition must be the guide. The doing must be done to learn. Drawing a design on a sheet of paper will not make a pot or any other ceramic piece. It can only be a point of departure. As has already been stated, there is the character of the material available to be contended with and the fact that the article is three-dimensional. No drawing can fully describe these. A design is a highly intellectual feat, but clay making presents problems and stimuli which are not so much intellectual as intuitive. The design fully suggests itself only when the clay is manipulated and the restraints and liberties to be taken with it become evident.

Look at some of the tortured pieces of pottery which are made. Obviously the design was first conceived by a non-clay worker. It was up to the poor potter to try and force his reluctant material to assume the shape. No drawing can ever impart the tactile value of the piece, nor determine the exact effect of the fire on the appearance of the glaze.

It has been said that the solid is the piece; the captured force the shape; the emotion the colour; the sensuality the feel; the intellectuality is in the function; and the aesthetic is the complete harmony of all, in the manner it has been done.

The actual physical nature of design varies according to the way space is conceived at any one particular time. A study of the art of primitive man shows he designed what he was acquainted with rather than what he saw at any one given instance. The shapes he conceived were free and not under the influence of any particular framework. Unlike modern western man, primitive man was not much concerned with the vertical and horizontal, or the mathematically equal division of areas. He drew an animal's guts with the same emphasis with which he drew its exterior. Australian Aboriginal decorations wander freely on the surface and the divisions are rarely if ever repetitively even.

About the time of Christ, pottery in all its forms was being made with a free vigorous strength for household or religious purposes in most parts of the world. In mediaeval times these qualities increased and gave us a virile tradition. Mass production brought about general lowering of standards. Clay was used like wood, metal or stone and aborted into unnatural productions. Designers imitated Asian and Greek pottery without understanding or taste, and our immediate ancestors had their pottery presented to them in many unnatural clay forms. Fortunately, it recently became the policy for industrial designers to work in the medium in which they were to design. As a result of this there has been a sudden raising of standards in work all over the world. Conception of form is influenced by the material and function. Much fine art pottery being made uses simple, balanced proportions and restrained glazes in functional shapes. Another strong trend is in free, sculptural, non-functional forms.

When considering design, return to nature for ideas. Study the stones shaped by water in watercourses and on the seafront. Look at the way melons, gourds and other vegetables and fruits swell from inward growth. Try to understand volume, the pressure of growth, disposition of weight, the sagging swell, or explore ovoid shapes. Study the alternatives of flat opposed to round, straight to curve, rough to smooth, cool to warm. Notice how one of these factors dominates, and the other complements the form or design to arouse interest. In every form the negative is of equal importance as the positive. What use is a wine jar without the space which holds the wine? The hand needs the hole formed by the handle. Space which surrounds form, showing off its character, is as important as the solid mass. Try to design from the centre of the volume working outwards rather than with outline. An eye is bored by a task too easy to solve. Pass a hundred posts evenly apart and the eye will scarcely see them. If one is missing or one is closer to the others, it immediately registers. The same applies to ceramic design. Give the eye an uninteresting, obvious shape and it is bored. Yet a very simple shape of subtle proportional relationships will hold interest.

If a design is functional, consideration must be given to the demands of the function. A teapot spout should pour cleanly. A teacup should keep the tea warm, but the handle should be cool and easy to hold. A salt shaker should be easy to fill and not clog in wet weather. In all these cases, the nature of the material will dictate some of the details of the shape.

Another consideration will be where the object is to be used. A casserole may need a flat profile to fit in an oven. A jug may be too long and thin for the part of the refrigerator available for it. The foot of an ashtry should be smooth so as not to scratch a polished table. Similarly, a jug must be easy to clean and a vase able to stand in a strong wind. The ware's function always affects the type of clay and glaze desirable. When all these factors are considered, a compromise may be necessary to balance function and design. Most cultures have been prepared to sacrifice function for beauty – although this has largely been governed by the character of the people.

Of course, many ceramic forms may have no precise function at all. They may be purely decorative – wall or garden ornaments, sculptural forms – forms designed to give pleasure to the eye or the touch.

Whether your design is functional or not it must be highly individual. When an approach is forced, because it is 'the thing to do', boring results can be anticipated. Design expression should be natural and unforced, within the capability and understanding of the moment. Small enjoyment will be gained by being somebody else. The problem is to find oneself.

design A

top left: Objects such as this stone suggest form and texture. Nature will provide further inspiration.

right: Examples of the manner in which a basic idea can be executed.

design A

design B

top: Functional forms for household use.

bottom: A coffee table with a top of moulded stoneware tiles. It is functional as well as being attractive.

161

A coffee pot illustrating the use of
a felspathic glaze with an iron
oxide decoration.

This plate and ashtray show the effects of using a dolomite glaze on an iron glaze with a wax resist decoration.

slip on clay

Slips made with clay and water (which must shrink at about the same rate as the main body) may be applied by dipping, pouring, trailing, brushing, pouring on mesh, applied with a palette knife or any other way which may suggest itself to the imagination of the potter. Slips are usually applied in a thick cream-like mixture.

These slips may be coloured with oxides to contrast or harmonize with the body of the pot. Coarse ingredients such as grog and sands may be added. They are usually applied to the pot just as it is made or when it is leather-hard. If they are used on dry or biscuit ware the plastic ingredients are calcined. Wax-resist decoration may be used with slip decoration to create a design.

right: An example of a slip being poured onto a slowly rotating pot.

top: Here the slip is settling down to form the decoration.

bottom: The finished pot.

The use of a thin dolomite glaze over a shiny iron glaze, with copper and ilmenite resulted in the attractive finish of this plate.

textures applied to surfaces

Textures may be applied to clay with the use of an open woven material, such as onion sacking, mosquito netting, dish cloth and any similar material. The material should be slightly dampened so it will cling to the pot.

top: A damp open-weave cloth is wrapped around a bottle.

bottom: The clay is then pressed through the mesh as required.

textures applied to surfaces

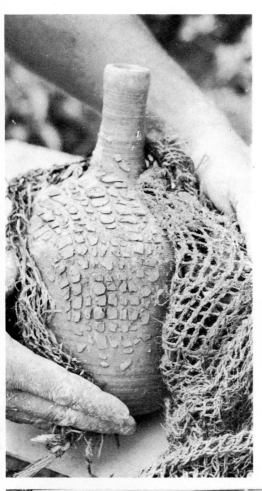

top left: The mesh is carefully removed and the texture is revealed. If some of the clay pulls off with the mesh, place the mesh back on the pot surface and apply some more clay. Dampen the finger and round any rough or sharp edges. Tap down any loose pieces onto the surface. The coarser the mesh used the higher the decoration will be on the surface.

top right: Wheels used to create patterns. The very touch of the fingers or the cut of the turning tool will give a texture which is sufficient in itself.

bottom: Further decoration can be gained with common household objects such as points, cords, clay stamps, wire loop tools, applied in an infinite number of ways. Glaze usually pools in the impressions or pulls away from the edges to emphasise the design.

This plate is a fine example of
decorative glazing by Len Castle.

removing clay (intaglio) and brushing on pattern

The surface of the clay may be incised by using loop-ended tools, points, combs and anything that will cut the surface.

top: Loop-ended tools are best for grooving. Points tend to score with furrowed edges, unless the clay is firm.

bottom: In some designs the clay may be perforated with holes or patterns. Designs may be drawn on the surface. The clay around them is removed to give a low relief decoration. When the clay is leather hard it is ready for this type of decoration.

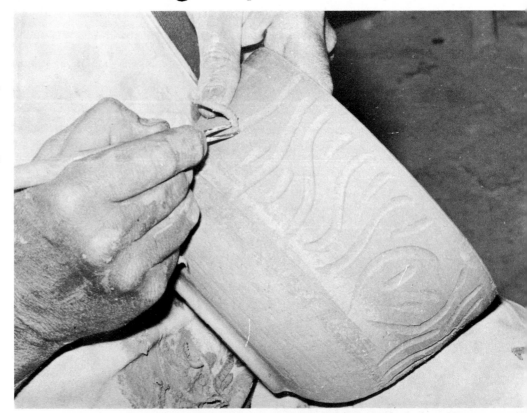

The pattern in this large bowl was
derived by using black oxide and
iron brushwork on felspathic glaze.

These plates and tiles show the effects of applying poured and brushed glazes.

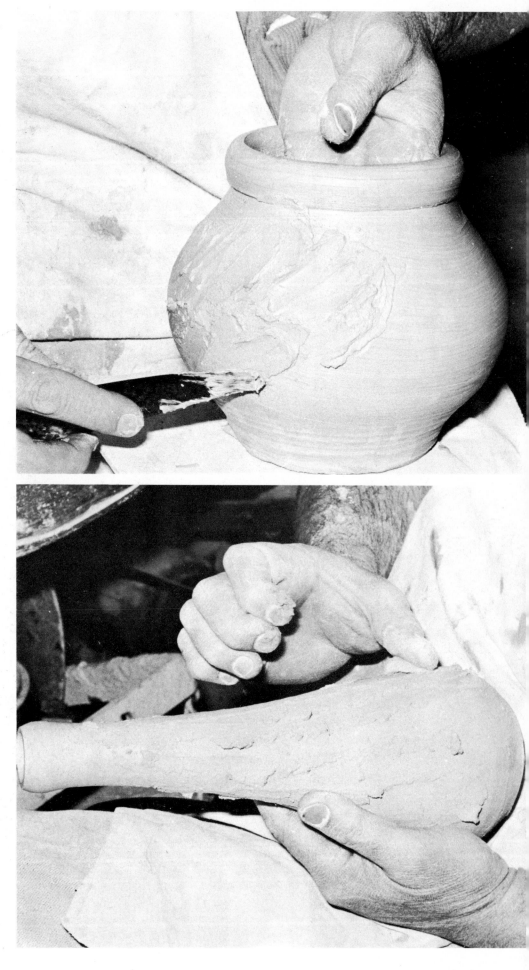

top, bottom: When the clay is damp, a clay of similar consistency is used for application and can be firmly pressed or smeared on the surface.

paddling

top: A basic shape may be given more interest by beating or paddling. The main shape should be finished to its final thickness as soon as possible so that it is still plastic enough to be paddled.

bottom: An ordinary wooden spoon may be used and the pot soon changes its shape. Working around the form gives a greater emphasis on bulk, working up and down for profile and rhythmic form. Clay may be added to the form and beaten in. Textures can be gained by using paddles with embossed surfaces.

6

colour

general

During all his known history, man has always felt the need for the use of colour and adornment. In the decoration of pottery, primitive people have used the ochres found within clay bodies giving a simple colour range. Some of these people also introduced brighter colours made from vegetable stains fixed with resinous substances applied after firing. As knowledge grew, impure metallic oxides were used to give a variety of colours. Most early Chinese pottery was coloured by the use of only iron or copper, with cobalt being introduced later. Modern technology has given a practically unlimited palette to the potter. But its use is of dubious benefit to the artist-potter.

For the very reasons the technologist rejects the use of various materials the artist-potter accepts them. Standardized mass production requires rigidly defined, highly refined and controlled colours. But, in most cases, these colours lack charm and variation of the oxide in its near raw state. The partly controlled result gained from the cruder materials, as often as not, makes a further statement which adds to that of the potter. The commercial colour has the acquiescence of a 'yes-man' with about the same interest. Some commercial colours are useful, however, to add subtle variations to oxides. Although many experiments in the use of bright colours are made by the student, his ultimate choice will usually be the oxides which seem to harmonize so well with the nature of clay and stone.

The use of the clay itself as a means of expression must first be considered. The fired surface of many clay bodies have sufficient colour, and textural interest to be left unglazed, at least in part, or revealed under a transparent glaze.

Oxides may be added to the clay to vary the body colour. Speckled effects may be gained with manganese and ilmenite. White or coloured grog will add a further character. The potter will find metallic filings, and other minerals may fire to some advantage in the body. The hue and tone of the oxides is effected by the quantity used, the colour of the clay body, the nature of the glaze and the temperature and atmosphere of the kiln.

To have a conception of the palette available, metallic oxides such as iron, copper, cobalt, manganese and chrome may be mixed with water and applied in cross hatched stripes on a clay form, preferably having both vertical and horizontal surfaces. This can then be biscuited, glazed and fired. If these test pieces have a hole in them they can then be hung on the studio wall for visual reference. This can be done with the oxides related to the glaze by being under, in and on it, and glazed by the selected glazes in use in the studio. Of course, only experience will show the proportions in which the colours can be used to best advantage – the proportion of warm to cool, dark to light, liquid to stable and so on.

You can also experiment with the effects gained by firing the clay in different ways. By oxidizing, you can produce one colour from the oxide. By *reducing* (removing oxygen) you can produce another colour from the same oxide. Different glazes will give varying results from the same oxide. Minerals such as zinc, nickel, silica, or zircon will effect the nature of the colour. It is from this knowledge that skill is acquired to express the use of colour in a personal way.

The most illuminating and dramatic way to observe the change of colour in the kiln is by Raku firing. Here the piece may be seen as it comes from the kiln after being fired in oxidizing conditions. It rapidly cools when the door is opened and the colour of the oxide appears. When a piece is removed and dropped into water the oxidized colour results.

It is even more dramatic when a change of colour takes place before your eyes. Take a piece from the kiln and place it in sawdust or leaves to form a local reducing condition – where the material covers the glaze. Copper greens change to red, gold and black. Iron deepens in red or turns green. In no other way can the conditions which cause the change of colour be seen so clearly. In all other forms of firing these changes occur in the kiln.

There is often no resemblance between the oxide and its final colour. Many oxides may be black in their original form. If they are coloured, they may transmute to another colour. Tin or zircon can be used to provide an opaque white. By using large quantities of some oxides you can obtain blacks or dark greys. Mixtures of oxides will also cause these dark tones. Other useful oxides are the mineral sands ilmenite and rutile, which will give browns and tans. Rutile will transmute to blue under certain conditions, when used in a glaze as a colourant in reducing fire.

Colour depends on intuition. Thousands of words will not help this innate sense of the creator. The conception must arise from within. The state of mind which creates is purely individual. It must be explored from within the individual and not from without. Influence and guidance may be sought from that which has been done. But if the final statement is to be valid, it must be purely personal. The personality is expressed in the manner of application. Some potters use carefully scumbled effects – that is they overlay liquid clay of different colours. Others use free brush forms in underglaze or oxides mixed with glazes. Some make deliberate or free incisions through clay or glaze, while others employ simple or multi-layered, sprayed effects. An uneven application of glaze will give varied surface qualities.

Experimenting with these techniques will suggest an infinite number of design and colour combinations.

These proportions, and the resultant colour, depend mainly on the factors of firing and glaze. Tests should be made to check the result. Many tones are made by inter-mixture. As the oxides may be applied in many ways, examination should be made of these.

vehicles or mediums for applying colour

The simplest application of colour is to slip-coat the piece with coloured clay. Slip, or liquid clay, is usually applied to the leather-hard ware, but may be used on bone dry pieces. If the slip has the same shrinkage as the leather-hard ware it will hold well. If it shrinks to a greater extent than the piece, some silica or similar filler should be added. When the slip shrinks less than the leather-hard piece, it may be used on bone dry pieces.

Thickness of application is governed by the desired effect and the ability of the slip not to crack if applied very thickly. Some slips are applied in thin washes, and covered with clear glazes to reveal delicate decoration. Others are layered to present textural effects.

The distinction between the terms 'slip' and 'engobe' is small. But engobe is usually taken to mean a compounded slip of finer quality material than that of the piece which it covers. It is often used on dry or biscuit-fired pieces. Compounding an engobe conforms to the same rules as making a slip. Such a compound can consist of a clay, flux, filler, hardener, opacifier and colouring oxides. Water is usually used as the medium for application. Applying the engobe at the leather-hard stage is, perhaps, the easiest, and gives greater versatility, allowing graffitto, that is encising through the engobe coat, to reveal the under surface.

A common engobe composition for this is-:

Kaolin	25 per cent	Silica	20 per cent
Ball Clay	25 per cent	Zirconium	5 per cent
Feldspar	20 per cent	Borax	5 per cent

For application on dry surfaces the clay content should be halved. Quantities of oxide for colouring are approximately the same as in the list on page 184. Many combinations of these oxides may be made to various shades.

Application may be made in many ways such as dipping, pouring, brushing, spraying, sponging, slip trailing and so on. Wax resist may also be used. The stronger oxides in engobes may bleed through white and opaque glazes, usually in an attractive manner.

Underglazes are laid much the same as watercolours in a direct, fluid manner, and usually under a transparent glaze. There is nothing to prevent their use in or on glazes. Simple underglazes may be made with oxides, water, glycerine or gum. Clay may be added to help prevent the colour running. Commercial underglazes are prepared in great numbers. Reliable manufacturers define the limitations of the colour with kiln temperature and atmosphere, but all should be tested. These underglazes

This jar shows the transmutation
of the warm colour of rutile to
that of a cool blue-green, by
means of reduction firing.

A shallow plate in warm earth colours.

usually consist of an oxide, flux and filler specially compounded, calcined and ground to prevent running. If the colour tends to make a glaze crawl, add some *frit* (see Glossary of Terms) to the colour, or apply it more thinly.

The glaze itself may be coloured with oxides, underglazes or a similar commercial stain known as 'glaze stain'. Incomplete mixing may add interest. Some oxides will cause the glaze to run. If a test indicates that this will happen, some calcined clay should be added.

Colour may be brushed, sprayed or poured on top of a glaze. In pouring a double layer of coloured glaze only minimum time should elapse between applications to prevent lifting through shrinkage.

Glue may be added to prevent damage when handling. A light spray of glaze over the decoration will also do the job. This is of help if the colour is rather refractory and coarse to the touch after firing.

Oxides mixed with a stable glaze such as grass ash, of a different quality to the dipped glaze will give contrast and depth. Incised patterns may be made through an oxide sprayed over the glazed ware. Glaze deliberately applied roughly, or in runs may be side sprayed, and the rough ridges dusted with a fine dry brush to gain character. Wax resist can also be used. An oxide or coloured glaze may be brushed or sprayed over the base glaze. Matt iron glazes usually brush and sit well on top of another glaze.

These applications can continue endlessly, and forethought should be given to the final aesthetic result. Here the potter is on his own.

a guide to proportions of oxides for colour

The oxides which colour the neutral tones of the base glaze are in addition to the original formula of the glaze. Therefore their percentage is described as 'by addition'. As the proportions of colouring oxides vary considerably to attain the tone and hue desired the convenience of this practice will soon be recognized. In some cases a number of oxides must be used to obtain a colour.

Tests should always be made before making large quantities of coloured glaze. The oxides added may act as a flux on certain glazes, and the addition of clay may be necessary to counter these fluxing effects.

In this general guide given below, the colours may be used for either oxidising or reducing firing unless stated otherwise.

BLACK
An overload of cobalt, iron, copper, manganese or ilmenite will give black.
A combined 2 to 3 per cent of any three of these oxides will be suitable.

A combination of
$\begin{cases} \text{cobalt 1 per cent} \\ \text{iron 8 per cent} \\ \text{manganese 3 per cent} \end{cases}$

WHITE
Six per cent of Tin will give a dense white.
As tin is expensive, many potters use 8 per cent zirconium. The mineral sand companies can supply micro-mesh Zirconium, which is most suitable.

YELLOW
Low toned yellowish hues can be gained by the use of rutile and dolomite in reduction firing only. Six per cent Vanadium gives yellow when oxidising firing.

GREEN

Copper, 1 to 5 per cent, fires to green in an oxidising fire.

Chrome at 2 per cent, and iron at 1 to 3 per cent will give green.

BLUE GREEN

A combination of $\frac{1}{2}$ per cent Cobalt and 2 per cent copper will produce blue-green when oxidising firing. If reduction is chosen $\frac{1}{2}$ per cent Cobalt and 1 per cent Chrome should be used.

BLUE

When the powerful colourant cobalt is used here $\frac{1}{4}$ to 1 per cent is needed. Small additions of iron, or other oxides will modify the characteristic hardness of this oxide.

RED

Rich, low toned reds are made with 5 to 10 per cent iron. The transmutation of copper in reduction firing results in red, using $\frac{1}{2}$ to 1 per cent.

TAN

is gained with 2 per cent iron, fired in an oxidising atmosphere, or 5 per cent Rutile in either fire.

BROWN

A warm red brown can be created with 4 to 6 per cent iron with an oxidizing firing. A rich speckled brown will result using 3 to 5 per cent Ilmenite in a reduction fire.

5 per cent manganese in either oxidizing or reduction fire will produce another shade of brown.

A bottle after being treated with a Raku reduction fired glaze with copper transmutation.

7

glazing

The glazes transmuting as
reduction takes place.

The kiln door showing the matured
ware, with molten glaze, ready for
removing from kiln.

left: Ware taken directly from kiln and being 'reduced' in sawdust.

bottom left: Ware being removed from sawdust heap after glaze transmutation has occurred.

bottom right: Dipping reduced ware into cold water to cool.

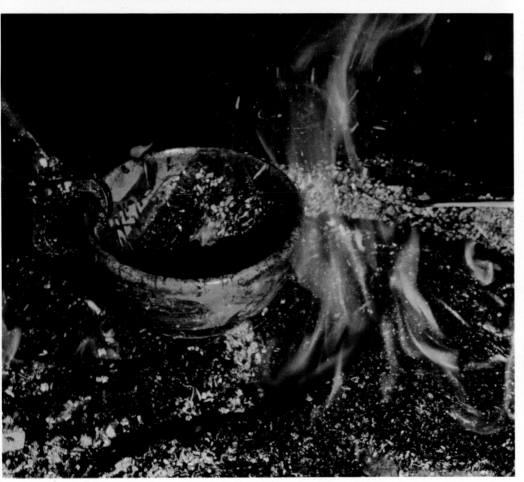

general

A glaze can be a moment of frozen beauty .... a liquid held in suspension for time infinite. Stoneware glazes have a unique character not obtainable in the glazes of other types of pottery. By the very use of partly refined materials, results of unique quality occur. At times, by some freak of the fire, they can be breathtaking.

The function of the glaze dictates its type and manner of use. If the piece is solely decorative, anything goes. If function is a factor, consideration should be given to this restraint.

Commercial pottery has adopted the expediency of uniformity. The materials used in its creation are refined and selected for a positive result – conformity to a standard. Creative pottery has no such restraint and may be as fine or coarse as desired. So with the glaze. Effects which would send a commercial potter screaming because they upset his preconceived ideas may be of interest to the artist-potter.

Most beginners, as beginners always will be, are interested in the most bizarre and complex combinations of glaze. As wisdom grows with experience, the beauty of limited means becomes apparent. Simplicity of form and glaze gives a strength and beauty not found in most overstated and overglazed shapes. An interesting exercise is to overstate and gradually reduce the decoration and glazes to the simplest statement.

The glaze is made of various minerals suspended in water. When a glaze is typed, it is usually typed by its chief fluxing agent. Commonplace local materials may be used, and refinement often only robs the glaze of character.

The ware is 'raw' in its clay state, or 'biscuited', by a low preliminary fire. Biscuited ware is easier to handle when glazing and loading into the kiln. Once fired pottery usually has a better fitting glaze and a different character. It is more suitable for slip decoration and work with surface qualitites which the potter wants to emphasize.

methods of applying glazes

Dipping is the most used method of glazing. The article is first cleaned and then plunged into the liquid glaze. It is removed in such a way that it has a fairly even covering of glaze. Keeping a desired thickness of glaze is the problem. The answer is judging the thickness of the glaze to the absorbency of the piece. If a piece is large, either the glaze should be thinned with extra water until it lightly covers the hand when dipped in, or the ware should be wetted so that it will only accept a certain amount of glaze. Only experience will show how this is done. If two or more glazes are superimposed, obviously the first glaze or glazes should be thinner. Also in this case, it may be necessary to add glue or clay to help bind the glaze to the piece and prevent crawling. Crawling is the state when the glaze peels back in parts during firing to reveal the clay surface. It is caused in this case by the second glaze cracking the adherence of the first glaze to the ware as it shrinks over it after dipping. Do not leave this further dip too long after the first has been done.

If the ware is being once fired it is imperative that dip glazing be done at exactly the right time in order not to crack the piece. This state on most clays is slightly drier than leather-hard. But it can be even drier according to the body used. The glaze must have sufficient clay in it to shrink with the clay body, which will have slightly expanded during the dipping procedure. About thirty five per cent clay or ten per cent bentonite is a rough proportion.

Slip glazing may be used. In this case, a clay which melts at a lower temperature than the maturing temperature of the kiln, or a clay with fluxes added to it so it will do this, can be used. This type of glazing is common in Asia. If this glaze cracks and peels off the ware, the clay for it can be *calcined* – that is fired to about red heat and then ground if necessary. This method will solve this problem.

For dipping you often need enough glaze in which to dip a fairly large article. As this is not always possible, you may have to make use of other methods of glazing.

Brushing is one such way. This should be done quickly on a slightly wetted surface to prevent too great a build up of glaze. It is an excellent method of glaze decoration.

Pouring is faster and more versatile. Once again, if the biscuit ware is dampened, greater control may be attained to prevent 'build-up' of glaze. Fast, sure action is essential to gain an even coat. With many glazes, an uneven surface can be very attractive, showing the run lines on the surface in whatever direction the glazer decides. A spray of oxides from one side to shadow and emphasize may further enhance the glaze. Pouring gives many opportunities for decoration over another glaze. When pouring a glaze, watch the 'build-up' on the edges. Dampen the edges well and they will repel some of the glaze and so remain fairly even. If they are slightly thin, it is a simple matter to brush a little more on once the glaze has dried. A flexible wrist, a brave pouring hand and a slightly damp surface are the best ingredients for the success of poured glazes. Sprayed glazes are most suitable for once fired pottery because the wetting qualities are reduced to a minimum and the thickness of glaze may be layered at will.

Many ingredients of stoneware glazes are harmless. But copper carbonate, barium carbonate, manganese and others are not. Dusts in a pottery are positively harmful to the lungs. It is essential that a fan should be used with indoor spraying to exhaust these fumes from the building, or a mask should be worn.

Always spray first the parts that are most difficult to reach, because it is impossible to tell how thick the glaze is on the piece once a coat of spray is on it. Inevitably, it is the awkward spots which are thin. A good memory and a work procedure method are necessary for full even coverage.

Instruction on 'feathering' the spraygun to obtain an even coat can be gained from the agent. These are the main methods of glaze application, and any others are minor techniques such as using a sponge, a roller and so on.

In all cases, the thickness required can only be known from practice, because the glaze may be so thin as to merely seal the clay, or so thick to be as unctuous as the impasto of an oil painting. Some glazes will run exceedingly or craze if too thick. Others are dry and uninteresting if too thin. When double dipping is used, only knowledge of the glazes will prevent the catastrophe of putting a runny glaze on an easily fluxed base glaze. Glazes which are indifferent on their own sometimes work well one over the other. Stable glazes are the godsend to the potter, but fluid glazes will often be the ones which give the heavenly results.

preparing different types of glazes

The materials required to make glaze will be containers, sieves of about sixty and one hundred mesh, fly screen, rubber gloves, dippers, scales, water and the glaze ingredients, and a felt ink pencil to label the container. The scales should have a sizable tray to hold the ingredients. Estimate the required quantity of dry ingredients to make sufficient glaze to fill the container. About five pounds of dry material are used to a gallon of water. The solids are always added to the liquid, and 'difficult' ingredients such as talc, ash and clays which need wetting are weighed out and added first, or mixed well with the other ingredients dry. These should not be disturbed as they are wetting, but insoluble materials such as silica and feldspar can be placed on top of them to push them under the water. If need be, add an excess of water to allow easy initial sieving. This excess is easily decanted later. Sieve several times if a harmonious blend is desired.

One of the advantages of high fired pottery is that the glazes can be made of simple local materials. There are many common substances which will melt to a glass at temperatures of 1200 to 1300 degrees Centigrade.

The simplest of all glazes are slip glazes which have been described. Many common red clays are suitable for such a glaze. If it is to be applied to the raw ware, it should shrink at a similar rate to the leather-hard pot. If it should crack off, then it may be necessary to calcine the clay over 600°C. It may need to be ground after this process, but it will then act as any dry inert glaze and can be used on biscuit ware. If the clay does not melt to a glaze at the temperature fired to, a flux can be added. Most of the early Asian glazes of this type were done with common red clays. The manner of application and firing gives the variation of results. These glazes are usually in the brown and red-orange colours. But oxides may be added to vary the colour. A good slip glaze will also increase the mechanical strength of the body from fifty to a hundred per cent.

Salt glazes evidently originated in Germany. This type of glazing is simple and quietly attractive. Colours can be applied to the ware as underglaze and these will show through the glaze. With the addition of about equal parts of borax, this type of glazing can be done as low as 900°C. with some success. But, a temperature of over 1200°C. is desirable for best results. In stoneware firing, the salt, often in the form of wet coarse rock salt, is added near the burners at about 1250°C. in a reducing atmosphere. It may be necessary to *bait* (throw in salt) three or four times. As each lot of salt is thrown into the fire, the temperature will fall. This should be allowed to rise again before further baiting. The use of up to fifteen per cent borax or boric acid, particularly in the last baiting will improve the glaze. The salt is vaporized and will cover everything in the kiln. The shelves should be painted with kiln-wash. As the kiln has continued salt firings, the residue on the walls will vaporize in firing with the result that less salt has to be added. The fumes from the kiln are dangerous and should be exhausted from the building if the kiln is inside.

Test rings may be placed near the spy hole from where they can be hooked out and examined to check the glaze thickness. The vapour from this glaze may not find its way into shapes like bottles and vases, and these may need to be glazed in these parts before firing.

Once a kiln is used for a salt glazing, the inside of it is coated with glaze. In an electric kiln this is disastrous. If it is desired to fire some salt glazed pieces without ruining the kiln for other work, this can be done by firing the pieces in a sealed *saggar* (a refractory box) which has its inside coated with salt and borax. The vapour caused by these ingredients volatilizing will coat the ware thinly.

Consideration will now be given to stoneware glazes which are applied as definite coatings on the ware, and fired between 1250 and 1300°C. A reducing atmosphere induced between about 1100 and 1250°C. with at least half an hour oxidation at the end of the fire is usually an excellent manner of firing these glazes.

One of the most interesting fields of glaze is that of ash glazing. Ash from vegetation contains all of the ingredients for glaze, but of course not in a balanced manner. These ingredients include potash and soda. Potters with tender skins should wear gloves. This ash also contains amounts of alumina, iron, calcium, magnesia, sodium, silica, phosphorous and other minerals.

In most cases, the larger the tree, the softer and more fluid the glaze. The hard stable glazes come from the grasses, including bamboo, rice, and wheat, they also come from fast growing weeds and shrubs, all of which are high in silica content. Ash glazes will vary slightly if the source of the ash is from different areas, because the mineral content of the vegetation will vary with the locality. So if an ash glaze composition contains fifty per cent hardwood ash, fifty per cent nepheline syenite or feldspar and three per cent bentonite by addition, the result may vary, even if the same tree ash is used. The larger and harder timbers of Australia yield a glaze that is generally of an opaque brown figlike colour, of soft appearance and fluid character. The fine ash of grass or pine is transparent, crisp, hard and stable. Ash glazes on their own cover a wide range and are usually easy to handle.

As a potter, one can become an excellent botanist, particularly if the local forestry department co-operates, as they will when they are thinning out forests or making paths, roads or fire breaks. At these times, if the potter is at hand, large quantities of ash are available, with the true botanical description of the tree. A positive enlargement of interest is evident in people who acquire a piece of pottery, with the further knowledge of its material creation.

A stable ash glaze, known as 'unctuous ash', should be fired at 1250 to 1280°C. It contains the following ingredients:

Potash Feldspar	50 percent	Silica	25 percent
Whiting	10 percent	Wood Ash	10 percent
Calcined China Clay	5 percent	Iron	1½ percent by addition

Ash glazes are most suitable for double dipping. They look well with a wax resist design. They lend themselves to further decoration, if desired, by the use of oxides mixed with them or sprayed or brushed on them. If the ash runs excessively, add calcined kaolin, by experiment, until the glaze behaves as desired.

Ash glazes are distinctive to stoneware and the character they have is sometimes exclusive to the neighbourhood in which they are obtained. Many ash glazes are extremely beautiful in their own right. If one should be a plain Jane, however, cosmetic aid may be applied with the addition of an oxide or another glaze. If the ash of old timber full of nails is used, the impurities from the iron may add an interesting speckled surface. A coarse sieve may be used. If a fine transparent ash from grass or pine is required, a fine sieve may be necessary.

Ash glazes may be made with clay and feldspar. One such glaze fired at 1250 – 1280°C. is as follows:

Ash	35 percent	Ball Clay	15 percent
Feldspar	35 percent	Talc	15 percent

If a running, overfluxed glaze is made, it can be used with discretion to make a fluid decoration on ware. Stable ash glaze with oxides added is useful for rigid formal design. When a glaze is dry, some ash added to it can bring it to life. Ash glazes each have their own individuality, and none quite conform to a preconceived idea. With a kiln test the nature of the ash in the glaze can be quickly observed and adjusted for the requirements desired.

In Asia, ash, feldspar, iron and common red clay were used to produce many glazes. Ash, feldspar and iron made many celadon glazes. Ash, lime, feldspar and common red clays were the base of the many variations of iron glazes used. These glazes remain practically unaltered today in Asia.

Iron matt glazes are most useful. They make a fine base for double dipping and also work well as a top glaze on a light base. For brushwork and edging other glazes, they are reliable in every way. One of these glazes most used in our pottery is fired at 1250 to 1280°C. If applied thinly over another glaze, a green hue is usually obtained. Its composition is as follows:

Potash Feldspar	60 percent	Whiting	2 percent
Calcined Kaolin	18 percent	Talc	15 percent
Silica	5 percent	Iron	10 percent by addition.

Another glossier version is fired at 1250 to 1280°C. Its composition is as follows:

Feldspar	45.1 percent	Calcined Kaolin	13.1 percent
Whiting	17.0 percent	Silica	22.6 percent
Zinc Oxide	2.2 percent	Iron Oxide	10 percent by addition.

If it should be needed, three per cent bentonite (with an equivalent reduction of kaolin) or some synthetic resin glue will assist to bind these glazes tightly to the pot. This glaze is not as stable a base as the previous one and double dipping should be done quickly, or these binders should be added to prevent the second dipping pulling the base glaze away from the pot and causing crawling. Of course the 'fault' of crawling can be very attractive if used in an organized manner, and any 'fault' should be observed, and the reason for its occurrence considered if it is suitable for interesting textural surface glazing.

Celadon glaze which gives colour from grey blues to green, gloss or matt, was mainly iron and wood ash as originally used in Asia. Many potters today use a feldspathic glaze as a base to make a celadon glaze and gain variety by adding iron.

1 – 3 % gives brown to treacly black
10 – 15 % gives metallic purple.

Generally the glaze is applied quite heavily. It is fired under reducing conditions subsequently oxidizing well at the completion of the firing to improve the glaze surface. Larger quantities of iron with perhaps some wood ash added, the glaze being heavily applied and fired under smoky reducing atmosphere, will give *temmoku* effects, browns and khakis changed to blacks and blues.

Many glazes can be made by adding iron, ochres, or the rutile-ilmenite family to various base glazes in different quantities and firing in reducing conditions of varying degree. Crudely prepared materials fired slowly under smoky conditions yield the most original results. Care must be taken when using iron as it tends to act as a flux and cause the glaze to run.

Feldspar is the most common flux used by the potter in stoneware firing. In Asia, simple feldspathic glazes were generally used when high firing was introduced. Some, it is said, were made only from feldspathic stone, or even parts of such natural feldspar and woodash. The use of local impure feldspars gave character to the ware of these potters and indicated the area of origin of the work.

One source of silica was ash of plants rich in this mineral, such as rice straw and fern-leaf. One such glaze fired at 1250 to 1280°C. consisted of:

Feldspar	20 percent
Rice Straw Ash	80 percent

Copper-red was achieved by using a copper slip under the glaze or adding copper to the glaze. Iron and other oxide-bearing minerals were used to vary the glaze.

The Western practice has been to use more refined materials in calculating glaze composition. There are hundreds of useful glazes. Study of other books on glazing will give many proven examples.

A fairly stable feldspathic glaze, clear at 1280°C. but milky if under-fired, is as follows:

Feldspar	44 percent	Kaolin	10 percent
Whiting	18 percent	Silica	28 percent

Limestone glazes are simple and beautiful. Usually they are composed from the maximum quantity of limestone able to be used. Whiting, a calcium carbonate, is used to supply lime. Firing temperature is 1260 to 1280° C. for these two examples. Use oxidizing or reducing fire.

EXAMPLE 1		EXAMPLE 2	
Silica	30 percent	Feldspar	80 percent
Whiting	25 percent	Whiting	20 percent
Feldspar	35 percent		
Clay	10 percent		

Dolomite or talc are two minerals usually chosen to provide the magnesia which makes the distinctive smoothness of magnesia glazes. Two examples are:

EXAMPLE 1		EXAMPLE 2	
Feldspar	25 percent	Feldspar	40 percent
Whiting	11 percent	Clay	15 percent
Talc	15 percent	Talc	15 percent
China clay	14 percent	Ash	30 percent
Silica	25 percent		

Fire between 1250 and 1280° C. Use oxidizing or reducing fire.

Matt glazes result when the glaze crystallizes. The term is used rather loosely in pottery, generally referring to a glaze with the minimum of reflective qualities. The simplest matt glaze is obtained by increasing the alumina (supplied by clay). Other matt effects can be produced by increasing the ratio of more refractory fluxes such as barium, lime and magnesia. Overloading the glaze with iron, manganese, zinc or rutile will give interesting matt crystalline surfaces.

The cooling cycle must be controlled. Slower cooling at the stiffening to freezing point of the glaze encourages these effects. Too fast cooling may give a bright glaze. Some kilns have a naturally slow cooling rate and crystallization is quite simple to achieve. Others will require some control through continued firing, but on a diminishing scale after the glaze maturity temperature has been reached.

While matt glazes are beautiful, some have a surface which may be unsuitable for some functions. Some give forth scratching sounds when eaten from with knife and fork and may be hard to clean. Two suggestions to be fired at 1250 to 1300°C. preferably by reducing fire, are as follows:

EXAMPLE 1		EXAMPLE 2	
Talc	30 percent	Feldspar	45 percent
Whiting	25 percent	Clay	25 percent
Feldspar	34 percent	Dolomite	25 percent
Silica	11 percent	Whiting	5 percent
Rutile	2 percent by addition		

The addition of twenty percent each of whiting and china clay to sixty percent glaze will perhaps produce a quiet matt surface. Tests will show which glazes work well and which become dull and uninteresting.

Opaque glazes are made by the addition of a substance to reflect light. The common minerals used are tin oxide and zircon, either alone or together. About five percent of tin oxide or ten percent of micro mesh zircon may be used.

Local rocks are a further interesting source of glazes. The material to make these may be obtained either in the field or by gathering it in the form of fine dust under machinery being used at quarries or masonry works for crushing or cutting stone.

While gaining experience, use the softer rocks which are easy to crush. The fine dust may be mixed with perhaps ten to fifteen percent bentonite which not only adds alumina to the glaze but acts as a binder. Wood ash may also be added to the glaze.

Suggestions to fire at 1280 to 1300°C. are as follows:

EXAMPLE 1		EXAMPLE 2		EXAMPLE 3	
Clay	15 percent	Clay	15 percent	Clay	15 percent
Rock	85 percent	Rock	45 percent	Rock	25 percent
		Ash	40 percent	Ash	60 percent

Take precautions against the glaze running when tests are being made.
Simple books are available giving the basic chemical composition of rocks, which will be a guide. Most departments of geological survey will supply fairly comprehensive maps of local areas showing known deposits of minerals and rock types.

A decision must be made whether to make glazes following chemical formulae, or by using natural materials by trial and error, with an intuitive, educated attitude. As the reader may judge, the prejudice of this book is slanted towards intuition. There is no need to copy slavishly the primitive Asian methods of glaze making. But observation of the character resulting from using readily available local materials which will easily form a glaze at stoneware temperatures between 1250 and 1300°C. suggests that by this very character the potter immediately has the opportunity of gaining an individual glaze to enhance his work. The refined materials will only repeat the glazes of everyone else who uses standard recipes. Further, the enjoyment and drama from the anticipation of opening a kiln and viewing a judged but uncertain result gives constant adventure to potting. Consider that most of the greatest Asian pottery of the past was produced by observation and deduction and that when the technique ceased to be a means to an end and became of paramount importance, the magic vitality usually vanished.

glaze faults

Glazes are composed of materials having varying expansion and contraction rates. The clay body also undergoes complex contraction while cooling. The potter aims to balance these factors to obtain 'glaze fit'.

CRAZING is the cracking of the glaze on the finished article. There are two sorts of crazing – 'immediate' and 'delayed'. Ideally, the body should contract very slightly more than the glaze, thus holding the glaze in a state of compression. If this is not the case, the glaze, being under tension, may craze immediately on being taken from the kiln. This crazing occurs because the glaze contracts more than it should. It may craze later if, for any reason, the body of the piece is to expand. For example, if it absorbs moisture it will craze even though this expansion may be very small. This is 'delayed' crazing. Crazing is perhaps best defined as tearing. This is most apparent in delayed crazing where the glaze is attached to the body. If the body expands, the glaze cannot expand to the same degree to stay with it and will consequently tear into fragments. The glaze will rupture first, because it is generally weaker than the body. On occasion a very strong thickly applied glaze will prove to be stronger than the body, and the body will shatter. As stoneware is usually vitreous, crazing may not be of major importance, depending on the aesthetic views of the potter.

SHIVERING is the opposite effect to crazing. In this case, the body has greater expansion than the glaze, contracting more and causing the body to shrink to a greater extent than the glaze can contract to. As a result, the glaze peels off or shivers. Shivering is generally attributed to excessive silica in the body. If silica has been added to the body, reduce the quantity. If the clay is naturally excessive in silica, add a less siliceous clay, add high-alumina grog, or use more feldspar.

The potter tries to tread the middle path. If crazing occurs, add silica to both or either the body and glaze, usually the glaze, in small additions. If any shivering results, then reduce the body silica slightly. A guide to follow is

> Not enough silica in glaze or body – crazing
> Proper proportions – sound glaze
> Too great a quantity of silica – shivering

CRAWLING is a condition where the glaze pulls back to reveal the body surface. This can be caused by glazing dusty or oily ware. Where an underglaze is applied too heavily, it may prevent the glaze adhering to the body. The glaze will then draw back off this surface during firing.

When a glaze is double dipped, or if the adherence of a base glaze on the ware is lessened through some cause, such as excessive shrinkage resulting from too much plastic clay in the glaze, it will crack and contract during the tensions of firing. This can be prevented by either cleaning the ware thoroughly, by adding calcined clay in the glaze or by adding a binder to assist adhesion.

Pouring a heavy glaze over a dry base glaze will break the adherence of the base glaze to the piece and cause crawling. When double dipping, apply the second glaze quickly before the base glaze is dry or add a binder to the base glaze.

RUNNING is caused either by a glaze being fired too high or applied too heavily. Either way, the glaze may run down to stick the ware to the kiln shelf. Altering the ratio between the fluxing and refractory parts of the glaze will rectify the first point. Heavy application is caused not only from having the glaze too thick, but not stirring it thoroughly, so that when the piece is dipped, one part is glazed too thinly and the other part has a heavy layer of glaze on it. Some glazes will act as fluxes to each other, so watch this when double dipping. Load the kiln where possible so that the variance of temperature in the kiln is in harmony with the type of glaze placed in each part.

DRY GLAZES can be rectified quickly by the addition of a quantity of suitable flux. Where the glaze has a rough surface from the use of refractory colours on it, a thin coating of glaze sprayed or brushed over the piece will make it more pleasant to the touch. If ware that is still damp from glazing is placed in the kiln and heat is rapidly applied, crawling or blistering may result.

There is a strong inclination to be disappointed with a glaze if it does not meet a preconceived notion, particularly when it is made from natural materials. Examine it closely and consider what other materials may be added to give it more character.

Deliberate use of faults is sometimes made. Blisters, deliberately or accidently produced, can be broken and lightly ground to remove the sharp edges. This gives an effect of moon-like craters. Crawling and crazing are used by some potters to gain effects.

Further faults, not connected with the glaze, may be caused by small pieces of refractory material dropping from the kiln roof or from under the kiln shelves. Brush these kiln surfaces well. If this does happen, often the offending material can be chipped or ground off, the flaw reglazed and the piece refired.

Be very wary of ware with weak sides near the base or other poor construction. This may encourage slumping in the kiln, causing two pieces to touch and fuse together.

Never fire untested clay or glaze. When glass is used in the ware, to make a heavy glass mass inside the piece, be sure the ware has a strong base. Otherwise the base may crack and the glaze run through. Many faults and uninteresting glazes can be cured with a second firing. Sympathy with the glazes and materials being used and intelligent pottery procedure will prevent most faults.

glazing a bottle

top: Some glaze is poured into the bottle.

bottom: The bottle is rotated as the glaze is poured out so that all the interior is coated.

top: As this piece is too large for the bucket, one end is dipped....

bottom left: ...... and then the other, the glaze is removed from the foot.

bottom right: Another glaze being poured onto the bottle after a wax design has been applied to one side.

201

glazing a plate

A method which may be used, if the glazes are of a type which can be applied thickly, is to rotate the shape on the wheel whilst pouring glaze. The speed of the wheel will cause various effects.

top: A thick glaze is poured onto a plate as the wheel is rotated slowly resulting in an even decoration.

bottom: Here an interesting effect is obtained as glaze is thrown at a high speed.

top left: Warm and cool. This effect is obtained by first a dark and...

top right: Then a light glaze being poured onto the plate. It is then rotated and flows into a free-form pattern.

bottom left: Here we see a glaze being poured over the underside of a plate. Rotation of the plate gives an even glaze.

bottom right: Pieces of broken glass are placed on the plate, these melt and form a thick multi-coloured glaze.

wax resist

A simple but effective means of decoration is the use of wax resist. In this example the piece is first brushed with a coloured oxide. Hot wax is then brushed onto the surface of the pot. The resulting design will resist (repel) the glaze when the piece is dipped.

top left: Mix iron oxide with water. Brush it on rather unevenly. Do not apply it so thickly that it will prevent the glaze adhering to the surface of the pot and cause crawling.

top right: Apply hot wax for the decorative linework.

bottom: In this example the pot is then dipped into a limestone glaze. In other cases the oxide will suggest the type of glaze to be used.

top: The pot is now ready for firing.

bottom: After firing the pot is completed. A limestone glaze on red oxide under reduction firing forms beautiful crystalline effect.

glazing implements

top: Holding tongs, dippers and gloves are useful aids.

centre: Brushes and sponges used during glazing.

bottom: This picture shows an ash glaze mixed with oxide being 'rolled' onto a pot, the brush is rotated between thumb and fingers.

top: When spray glazing, it is essential that an exhaust fan is used to remove noxious fumes from the workroom.

centre: Using tongs to dip ware.

bottom: Demonstration of thixotropic action which draws the glaze onto the piece. It should be noted that only the lightest touch is necessary to apply the glaze to the surface.

8

kilns

types of kilns

From primitive times, when humans first learned to harden clay by fire, many more kiln designs have been conceived than there is space in this book to describe. Even today, African women heap their handbuilt water and cooking bowls one on the other and fire them in the open with dry grass or maize to give a low-fired cheap and thermal shock resistant pottery of traditional beauty. Trench kilns and open walled kilns are also still in use, giving the further refinement of containing the heat to some degree.

Bank kilns may have been the next innovation. A chamber was built in the side of a hill through which the heat had to pass. This enclosed combustion chamber, with its primitive firebox and flues, gave the potter a kiln to reach higher temperatures. These kilns were up-draught kilns where the hot gases passed directly through the kiln. Much heat was wasted even though maximum use was made of skilful stoking and stacking. In Asia today, this type of kiln is still in use in a refined version. Connected chambers are built on the side of a hill. The heat rises through the chambers from the firebox at the lower end. The lower chamber is brought to temperature first and the others act as the chimney while also being preheated. One after another the remaining chambers are brought to maturity using stokeholes in their sides and then each is shut down. This routine gives even firing. Varying atmospheres may be used in each chamber for glaze effects. This kiln is also more economical on fuel, being traditionally fired with wood.

Most modern potters use down-draught kilns fired with wood, gas, coke, coal or oil. This gives maximum efficiency for a small intermittent kiln. There are many alternate designs, some of which will be described.

Electricity gives radiant heat, and many electrical kilns are built to give clean conditions of firing in any surroundings.

The best way to learn about kilns is to build a Raku kiln, and fire it. The construction is of loose bricks and the kiln may be easily rebuilt in many designs. It costs very little to build and fire. Other kilns discussed here will cost quite a lot, particularly when expensive refractory insulating bricks are used.

Fuel will be a major influence in deciding the type of kiln to build. Wood kilns will be impossible in a closely built area. In recent years, liquid petroleum gas has become readily available. This fuel is useful where town or natural gas is not available. In a built-up area, the choice will lie between electricity, gas, or liquid petroleum gas. In open areas, wood, electricity, liquid petroleum gas or oil can be used. The use of coke depends on the supply of a high class material.

Kiln construction can be of loose bricks as a Raku kiln is built, the fairly loose construction of a catenary arch kiln, or mortared brickwork, sometimes contained in a metal box. It is apparent with experience of building small kilns, the advantages gained by using refractory insulating bricks which are precise in shape, easy to handle and shape, and give such greater efficiency. They are more expensive than the common firebricks and often do not last as long. But these factors are outweighed by their advantages.

It is essential to know what results are desired before buying or building a kiln. Many amateur kiln builders, such as electricians or brick-layers or even 'handymen' making extra money may offer a kiln for sale. If the brickwork, burners, elements, and so on are not of a type to do the work, the kiln will soon burn itself out or work inefficiently. These kilns often have spy holes that are too small, no means for steam to escape during water smoking, weak arches which will not stand the expansion of high temperatures, insufficient heat input and so on.

Probably no kiln can be designed which has every quality. Different potters have various conceptions of the work they wish to do and the kiln must fit these demands. But, make sure the kiln, or the materials it is to be built of, fulfil its requirements by specifying its work such as 'firing to 1300 degrees Centigrade under oxidizing and reducing conditions, ten hours firing, fifty hours cooling and gas burning'. The material suppliers then have definite qualities to meet. For instance, some ceramic cements will not stand reduction firing and some bricks will not withstand direct flame impingement.

It is a further mistake to go to the opposite extreme and use materials of a quality made for much greater heat than that to be used. The suppliers will explain these are not ideal for many reasons. Much research and care has been taken to make specific qualities for the various temperatures.

Like any machine, it is important that replacement parts are readily available and easily installed. Standard kiln shelf sizes must fit the kiln design. Some expensive kilns are designed in such a way that a simple repair job, like replacing the floor, calls for the virtual dismantling of the kiln. Others have ridiculously deep firing chambers causing grave loading problems. These designs are usually done by engineers with an excellent knowledge of the use of heat, but little imagination for repair and working conditions. Tightly bonded brickwork not having expansion joints will cause cracking in the weakest parts of the kiln.

Considerable expansion will take place with high temperatures and allowance must be made for it.

If there is an area where one can be liberal it is with the supply of heat. A wood kiln with a firebox that is too small, a gas or oil kiln with small diameter pipes and an electric kiln with insufficient power input will all take a very long time to reach the required temperature. As long as delicate control can be kept, reserves of heat are desirable.

Provided the ware is not subjected to *hot spots* (greater heat in one spot), the type of firing being discussed in this book, can be fired openly without *a muffle* (protective space) or *saggars* (protective boxes).

Earthenware oxidized glazes using lead require a clean atmosphere. High temperature stoneware glazes are less fastidious, because lead is practically never used.

Insulation should be of a type which will minimize the loss of heat by insuring the prevention of the major means of heat dissipation, conduction and radiation – heat losses through the material, or convection losses through air spaces. An accepted practice is to use fine diatomaceous earth powder as insulation, because it meets these requirements. But the walls of the kiln are built slightly arched to withstand any inward pressure from the loose pack. Insulation is basically achieved by using the poor conductivity of air. Heat passes through solids by conduction, and through open spaces by radiation and convection. Loose diatomaceous earth ideally fulfils these requirements because of its fine, but porous grains. It can be kept loose to reduce conduction and radiation to a minimum. In one case, where a kiln was built on a slope, a load of ashes poured over it, except for the loading door and fire box, proved efficient insulation. Solid insulating concrete mixes and insulating brick are very good. But cracks usually appear which invite convection losses.

A recent product, insulating alumina – silica blanket sold as Kaowool, can be draped over the kiln's external surface to give excellent insulating qualities.

preparations for firing

top left: Shelves are dusted with fine sand to prevent the ware sticking to the shelf.

top right: A mixture of sand, kaolin and glue is brushed onto the edge of a lid to prevent sticking. It is fired in place on the bowl of the casserole dish. All glaze should be removed where surfaces touch.

bottom: A biscuit kiln stacked ready for firing.

main fuels:

GAS is easily controlled, and requires no hard work. The kiln can be left for known periods once its rate of climb is established. The flame is clean and firings can be done in confined spaces provided there is adequate ventilation and exhaust. Gas, in one of its types, is well worth considering even though it may not be the cheapest fuel.

ELECTRICITY gives heat by radiation and the results are visibly different from heat by combustion. An electric kiln can be burnt in the same conditions as a large kitchen stove, because the heat is contained in a well insulated box, and the controls are easy to manage and efficient.

The conditions in the kiln are always oxidizing, unless reduction is caused by dropping moth balls or pine slivers into the kiln at the required temperature. This operation will certainly effect the elements if they are on the inside of the kiln. It will probably remove eyebrows if the kiln firer is not careful.

Electricity is the most convenient of the fuels, but the firing results are limited. The advantages of the convenience will outweigh the defects to some potters when choosing a kiln. Do not wire an electrical kiln without technical assistance. It is dangerous and probably an offence under local law.

WOOD AND CHARCOAL

Immense satisfaction can be derived from the use of wood firing. The whole procedure is an artistic drama. Through knowledge one gains a sympathy with the fire and an ability to detect reasons for insufficient rise of temperature or poor firing conditions. It is also hard, tiring work to fire a wood kiln for twelve or more hours. One has to judge whether the sore eyes, tired muscles and soot and dirt are worth the results. Many potters think they are. There is no better way of finding out than to fire a Raku kiln and no lesson could be any cheaper.

For a stoneware firing a large quantity of wood will be needed. During reduction there will be large amounts of smoke and soot. It is advisable to have space and accommodating neighbours. You can obtain fuel from a wood cutter, timber mill or a furniture maker who will have offcuts. The fuel must have a high calorific value.

Ordinary firebricks rather than insulating firebricks are the best to use because there is considerable abrasion in this type of kiln, particularly in the general area of the firebox and bagwall. Every potter should try wood firing to learn lessons about the kiln that more sophisticated methods of firing will not teach.

OIL is used under air pressure with special burners or with simple drip feed burners by art-potters. Both forms of firing can yield smoke and soot if neglected. It was once thought that oil firing using pressure burners caused rapid deterioration of kiln walls. Later investigation has shown faulty firing was the main cause of this. Care must be taken to ensure an automatic cut off of oil if the air pressure ceases, because the burning oil, if unchecked, will stream on to the ground.

Many drip-feed kilns have been made and used. It is well to note that these should only be built in a large open area because copious smoke pours out from these kilns even, at times, after firing technique is achieved. The principal is to gravity feed oil to a burner which has natural draught or a simple forced draught system.

A simple example would be one having a drum of kerosene with a tap which can be adjusted to drip the kerosene down into a funnel on a pipe. The pipe has a goose neck in it to prevent flashback from the burner. It is attached to the burner which consists of a half inch water pipe with one thirty second of an inch holes spaced half an inch apart. The pipe is about a quarter of an inch off the ground. After preheating the pipe, the kerosene is lit and firing commences. The firehole can be covered with a steel plate drilled with holes, or a similar grill to further soften the flame. In this method hot gases pass over a bagwall into a five cubic foot kiln, through the floor and then into a chimney about thirteen feet high. The chimney which is adjustable need only be galvanised iron water pipe, this is economical and will last twelve months with moderate use. Ten feet is the ideal height for firing earthenware at around 1100°C and thirteen feet for 1300°C. But with a forced draught the chimney could probably be almost dispensed with. About four gallons of fuel will be consumed over six hours when firing to a temperature of 1300°C. A longer fire will give cleaner conditions and no smoke.

This is only one variation of this simple means of firing. Many other designs will work with the burners designed to have the oil dripping on a set of louvres in the fire mouth or specially made burners with air injecting to mix with and atomise the oil.

Many designs have appeared in 'The New Zealand Potter', which can be obtained from Box 12–162, Wellington North, New Zealand. The Japanese have several simple and cheap units for oil burning on the market with burner and blower set-up in one unit.

Whichever kiln is decided upon, become knowledgeable about its character and work within these limitations. With one or two clays, several glazes and oxides and a good kiln the variations of results are infinite.

a simple gas kiln

below: Here we see the kiln in the first stages of construction. Two layers of bricks have been laid to form the base and part of the walls have been constructed. The burner nozzle is level with the floor of the fire box and an area of sixteen square inches is left around the burner nozzle. Three inches have been left under the combustion chamber floor which still has to be placed.

top: A view of the kiln floor showing the space left for combustion. Just over two inches of space has been left between the floor and the back wall. Allowance is made for the pyrometric thermocouple to be inserted through the wall. More bricks have been laid. The door is shown.

bottom: Here is the finished kiln. The roof is supported by a tile. But these soft bricks could easily be drilled and supported by a rod, or put in as an arch. The pyrometer is inserted. The three protruding bricks form the door. The chimney flue is level with the top of the kiln, over the burner, its outlet is level with the floor. It is about sixteen square inches also. If unburnt gases can be smelt it must be enlarged.

top: Leave the door open and use a taper to light the kiln.

centre: This particular kiln was being fired for Raku and some of the pieces are shown being preheated over the top flue. The kiln has a very low gas consumption.

bottom: Ware with molten matured glaze is ready to remove from the kiln after Raku firing.

217

downdraught kiln fired with town gas

top left: Using insulating refactory bricks the construction is started in an old steel tank. Space is left between the bricks and the tank wall for powdered diatomaceous earth. The walls dividing the flues in the firebox are not yet installed.

top right: The walls are built. The arch, made of refactory cement is braced with bricks supported by angle iron on the wall. The protruding bricks in the wall are to support the bag wall which directs the flame to the top of the kiln.

bottom left: Old tiles have been used to form the bag wall. The floor is now complete, supported on the tiles which divide the firebox flues. Insulation is about to be laid over the arch.

bottom right: A biscuit kiln being loaded in the now completed kiln. The door is of loose bricks slurried over with sand and clay.

Town or natural gas in firing is perhaps the cleanest, most efficient and convenient of all methods to use. Construction is simple and the kiln can be fired to 1300°C. easily without the use of forced draught.

If the kiln is constructed between eight and twenty cubic feet the principles of building do not vary to a great degree.

In the design to be described below the only variations will be in the gas flow and chimney height. The larger the kiln the more gas that will be needed, therefore one or more extra burners will be necessary. A small kiln will have its chimney flue almost level with the crown of the kiln. A kiln with a higher firing chamber will need a correspondingly higher chimney.

Firing kilns of these sizes can be done in six to twelve hours depending on the capacity of the firing chamber and the load in the kiln.

According to cubic capacity four or five burners will be sufficient. These are alternatively placed – two on each side of the kiln.

Various types of burners may be used and an efficient type is a one inch low pressure gas inspirator at four inch water gauge. The kiln will have to be built inside a steel box if loose insulation powder is to be used. Further developments in insulation technique have resulted in the manufacture of a alumina-silica thermal blanket known as Kaowool, which is being used successfully in place of powdered insulation. A steel angle iron frame would still be necessary to brace the arch of the kiln to prevent its collapse during the expansion and contraction of the kiln firing.

High quality insulating refractory brick will prove economical and easy to use. Although this brick has a high initial cost, its insulating qualities will soon save on fuel consumption.

Denser bricks should be used where direct flame impingment occurs at the base of the kiln walls opposite the burners.

When powdered insulation is used (such as diatomaceous earth) an inward pressure will be exerted on the walls. Provision for this pressure should be made during construction by building the walls with a slight outward arch.

Smaller kiln walls should be built using the three inch side of the brick while larger kilns use the four and a half inch side of the brick.

Insulation is provided by nine inches of powdered insulation, or a recommended thickness of Kaowool blanket. The arch is constructed of insulating refractory bricks or cast in sections using castable refractory, three inches thick. Insulation is done to the same degree.

The doors are made with loose insulating refractory bricks using the three inch side. Any cracks are sealed with a slurry made with sand and a little clay to bind it. Further insulation is provided by another three inches of insulating brick.

One or more spyholes are provided in the door, these should be at least two inches in diameter to allow a good view of the pyrometric cones in the kiln.

Six inches of brickwork is needed under the fireboxes. The flame is channelled under the hearth through four-and-a-half-inch by four-and-a-half-inches flues. These flueways are divided from each other by one inch splits (thin firebricks) four-and-a-half-inches high. The walls so formed also support the kiln floor. The thickness of the floor is decided by experiment. Old cracked kiln shelves can often be used because they are well supported by these walls. A minimum space of two inches is left between the floor and the walls. This gives a space four-and-a-half-inches by two inches opposite each burner for the flame to enter the firing chamber.

Thought must be given to easy maintenance of this part of the kiln, as it is subject to the greatest wear. It should be built so that each part may be independently replaced.

Bag walls, (protective walls) are placed parallel to the sides of the kiln wall which directs the fire upwards to the arch. These walls can be made from old kiln shelves. They should not be fixed as this makes for difficult maintenance.

The outlet flues are at floor level. An even heat is gained if two, three inch square outlet flues are placed on each side of the kiln near the door, and a six inch by four-and-a-half-inch flue at the centre back. There are other ways of arranging these flue holes but their area must not be less than stipulated.

A hole for the pyrometer thermocouple may be provided in the back wall. Dampers are installed at the chimneys to control reduction firing.

a catenary arch
liquid petroleum gas fired kiln

For the non-bricklayer, a catenary arch kiln presents an answer in simplified brick laying, because most of the main structure is completed on a form which is later removed. Very little shaping of brick is necessary. Any practising potter will be impressed by the ease of building particulary when the time comes to replace the main section of the kiln.

When designing, keep in mind the sizes of shelving available, and the general size of the work to be done. This will suggest the dimensions of the internal space required.

The form of the catenary arch is defined by the curve of a chain passing through three given points. Draw on a wall the front plan of the setting space, including the protective bag wall, and a little space to spare. A chain can now be draped from two points representing the bottom of the sides of the kiln, and one representing the crown. Advice from the suppliers of the fuel to be used will indicate the necessary combustion space required between the setting space and the kiln walls. This will fix the point from the crown. The shape of the arch is described by this curve.

A wooden form is then made the full length of the kiln, but several inches inside the curve of the arch are left to allow removal of the form, which is wedged up during construction to the designed height. The kiln illustrations were built by Milton Moon. It is fired using natural draught. It has a capacity of twenty-four cubic feet, with a chimney seven-and-a-half feet high. The time to rise from cold to maturity of around 1300°C. is nine to ten hours, according to load, and whether in fact it is cold or still holds some heat from a previous fire. The total cost of building was about $A300

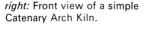

right: Front view of a simple Catenary Arch Kiln.

plus umpteen hours of hard work.

Three burners are used. They are simply constructed from pipe, with a bell shaped, perforated device on the end to adjust the pressure of the gas to the particular conditions. In this case the gas was adjusted to give a slightly lambent (lazy) flame rather than an oxidizing one, so that the gases would burn not so much in the fire box but in the kiln chamber where there was space for the gases to expand and where the heat was required.

The gases pass under the kiln floor, converging towards the centre of the kiln. Then they pass up behind a short, twelve inch bag wall around the arch and down to exit ports on each side of the flue where they have entered. The ware and shelf arrangement is designed to ensure this.

In the illustrated kiln, concrete was used only as a foundation from which to spring the arch. High quality insulating refractory firebricks were used on the inside, with only the top six shaped into wedges. Behind these is a layer of diatomaceous bricks, covered by commons (fire-bricks). The back and door of the kiln are made up of four-and-a-half inch insulating refractories and three inches of diatomaceous earth bricks. The door and arch of the kiln overlap to avoid loss of heat which would occur as the arch expanded. The chimney flue is at the top for maximum efficiency. The chimney is made from fire bricks. No metal bracing has been used on this kiln and it has not been found necessary.

This design can be used also for town gas, with slight alteration to the burners. It is also suitable for oil firing, always taking into consideration the different combustion spaces required. Wood firing can be done, usually by making two fireboxes and ash pits running the length of the kiln on each side of the setting space. When gas is used, the firing can be done without muffle or saggars.

left: Side view showing burners, firing is by liquid petroleum gas.

wood firing

Wood firing kilns are the pampered darlings of all kilns. They demand constant attention. The fuel must be cut to the right size and fed at the right time. There is also a considerable art in knowing which is the right size and what is the right time.

To become initiated into the mysteries and skills of wood firing, begin with a small kiln no larger than the one described in this chapter, or better still the Raku kiln, which is so cheaply built and fired. With a large kiln, and no skill, the potter may give up in despair of ever being able to reach the required temperature. A change of approach to the method of firing, the way the ware is stacked, the way the shelves are arranged, the use of the damper, the size of the fuel, and so on will assure the right temperature is reached.

Wood in many parts of the world is still plentiful and cheap, and often potteries are sited with convenience to fuel rather than to clay. The local wood supplier will be well aware of the wood with the greatest calorific value. Old time bakers and users of wood ovens will be able to tell of the best burning and heat-giving woods. Any forestry department will be of help here. The art of wood firing has a different atmosphere to any other. It is a more leisurely process and a much greater intimacy exists between the potter and his flame than in any other type of firing.

The potter will be watching the weather. The rise or fall of atmospheric pressure will have an effect on the firing. The kiln has a constantly changing personality, from the lazy quiet beginning to the dramatic climax of full fire, flame issuing from all ports, and greedy demands for fuel.

Following is a description of a typical firing of a simple twelve cubic foot downdraught wood kiln. The evening before the firing, light a small fire of chips at the front of the fire box. The door of the kiln has the top two courses of brick still off and the chimney flue is wide open. Keep the fire burning gently until bedtime. Rise early the next morning and commence the firing. If the ware is to be once fired, the firing must be slow and the top of the kiln door should be left open until colour appears in the kiln. If the ware has been previously biscuited before glazing, the evening in a warm kiln should have evaporated any moisture and the heat can rise as rapidly as required.

Commence firing with chips and several pieces of wood about one-and-a-half inches in diameter. After 100°C., fuel can be increased. When a glow eventually appears in the kiln, the doorway should be sealed. If the current of cold air passing through the kiln appears too strong, and is preventing the temperature from rising, then reduce the area of flue by partially closing the chimney damper. Watch the pyrometer to see if the adjustment caused a rise of temperature. Efficiency of the position of the damper can be checked by opening the top spy hole in the door then slowly closing the damper until heat is felt to exude from the hole. Slowly open the damper again until no heat is felt, and leave it at this point.

With once fired ware, red heat should be reached, so that all the chemical water is expelled from the ware before rapid increase in firing. The air passing through the firebox is blocked. All air now passes under and up to it through the ash pit.

From now, charge the firebox with wood about three inches in diameter. If the rate of stoking increases with no resultant rise in temperature, close the damper slightly. Observe that sufficient air space is left around the fuel so that ignition is at its maximum at all times. This basic rhythm is continued until about 1150°C. is reached. At this time, the temperature will tend to flatten out. Do not choke the firebox with too much fuel to counter this. Reduce the size of the fuel so that combustion will be faster and feed more often. Warm the timber by stacking it around the fire box. Ash is grey and is dull with air blowing on it. It should be raked out of the firebox as it is performing no useful function. Wood still being burnt may be thought to be ash. But if there is any colour in it it is in effect charcoal. It should not be disturbed, because it is still effectively creating heat. If this glowing ash falls into the ash pit, rake it to the front of the ash pit to form a mound of glowing coals to preheat the air passing over it as it enters the kiln.

Throughout the firing, rhythm is the basic technique. As fuel is thrown into the firebox a pattern of visible events will be evident. The addition of fuel will create the condition which results in reduction, shown by flame rising from the chimney. As the flame dies, oxidization is in process, and in a short time the fuel has been used and more is required. So a recurring pattern is apparent. Once the rhythmic timing is sensed, the adding of fuel becomes an easily defined system.

While the pyrometer shows a definite rise, and as long as the temperature is rising, do not overstoke. The flue under the fire grate and the chimney flue should be wide open. When the kiln temperature seems slower to rise, reduce the diameter of the wood to half an inch or an inch thickness. Fire like this until 1280 or 1300°C. is reached, or until the *cone* (a device for measuring the work done by the heat) appears ready to drop. A time of mellowing oxidizing conditions is now needed for perhaps half an hour. Open the damper and make sure no flame is showing at the spyhole or chimney. Stoke at a rate which keeps this clear condition.

Upon completion of firing, the firebox and chimney and other openings are entirely blocked after allowing about half an hour for any waste gases to escape.

The kiln has risen to 850°C during the first ten hours at about 80°C an hour. Once reduction becomes heavy, this rise drops to about 50°C an hour. This makes a firing cycle of about seventeen hours to reach 1280 to 1300°C. This cycle may be slower if desired. At least one whole day must pass before the door is slowly opened to unload. The usual cooling period is four times the firing cycle. All apertures are opened slowly when the kiln has cooled.

raku kilns

Traditional Raku pottery is very low fired earthenware. It is fired in a small kiln. Usually it is associated with making cups for the tea ceremony in Japan.

No more rewarding introduction to pottery can be found for the beginner. Every aspect of pottery is dealt with – preparing the clay, making the pottery, building the kiln and learning how to fire it, mixing glazes and learning how to use them. All this can be achieved in a few days. Of course, you may not necessarily be successful at the beginning.

The clay is usually a fire or stoneware clay, with at least twenty-five per cent grog, or as much as can be added without spoiling the workability of the clay. Any method of making may be used. After the ware is made and dried, it is biscuit fired at about 800–900°C.

Making the kiln is a simple matter and takes only about an hour the first time and once the principles are mastered it is a simple adaptation to vary the size of the firing chamber. About 150 full and thirty half bricks, (preferably fire bricks, but common bricks will do) will be needed for the design shown here. No mortar is necessary.

It should be noted that other fuel fired kilns can be used for firing Raku. The simple gas kiln previously described would be suitable.

Firing is a skill. A remarkably small quantity of wood will be used if it is done correctly. A little fuel is added often. For a beginning, a pyrometer can be used, if one is available, to gauge how effective the stoking is. Once the technique is mastered, the eye will become accustomed to the varying conditions and temperatures, and the pyrometer should be dispensed with. Fire with an eye on the top flue. If no smoke is visible, the kiln will be oxidizing. But no climb in heat may be evident because the draught may be inducing too much cold air into the kiln. A slight smoke will show near neutralizing conditions and a rapid gain of temperature will be evident. Smoke and flame will indicate reducing conditions. Fuel is being used to no avail. Observe the ashes in the ash pit. They will also indicate the condition of the fire.

The fuel for firing should be dry, light fast firing wood. Fruit cases or long thin offcuts from a furniture factory are ideal.

Skill must be acquired in firing. The first lesson to be learned is that only a small amount of fuel is used at any one time. It is not very important if too much wood is used in the early stages of the fire (to about 400°C.). From here to the mature temperature of 850 to 950°C. the secret is in the constant use of only two lengths of wood fed continuously into the fire box. The front part of the fire box is used to preheat the wood. The pieces of wood are spaced evenly and the fire concentrated under the fire-box. As the wood is consumed at the back of the fire box the preheated fuel is fed further in. There can be no lessening of attention, this procedure is continual.

Once mastered a steady rise in kiln temperature will be attained.

For handling the ware, tongs can be improvised with a cheap pair of pincers with eighteen inches or more of light metal tubing forced on the handles. Asbestos gloves will be necessary to protect the hands, and long-sleeved clothing of a non-inflammable type should be worn. When the glaze appears to melt, the tongs can be used to remove the pieces from the kiln. Some potters judge this condition by the reflection of the tongs in the glaze. A tin of water or cold tea nearby is used to drop the ware into to cool.

A smoky reduced effect can be gained by placing the piece into a tin with sawdust or leaves in it and then covering. If copper is used with the glaze, transmutation to red can be effected.

After the kiln is emptied a new load can be immediately added. But these pots must have been well pre-heated around the top flue. They can be stacked quite carelessly one on the other in the kiln, as the glaze will still be molten when they are removed and heal over any marks. Usually about fifteen minutes will bring the glaze to maturity, if the temperature is not lost during reloading.

Colour can be obtained with oxides under, in or over the glaze. Tin will whiten the glaze. Although raw lead glazes are widely used, it is best to use fritted lead or borax glazes, as the raw lead glazes are still soluble at these temperatures.

The following are glazes which mature between 850 and 900°C.

BORAX GLAZE:
Borax 70 per cent
Ball Clay 30 per cent

LEAD/BORAX FRIT GLAZE
Lead Bisilicate 16 parts
Borax Frit 4 parts
Feldspar 2 parts
Kaolin 1 part

Some gum may be added to the glazes if necessary.

In the United States today, Raku firing is being extensively used to fire sculpturesque shapes. Often the kiln it built around the piece. Raku pottery is inexpensive. The materials are easily available. Yet the results have an appeal which grows.

top: The base course is laid, with the bricks on their four-and-a-half inch side. One side is five-and-a-half bricks long, the back wall is one-and-a-half bricks long, the other side is five bricks long. The walls are nine inches apart. Normal brick laying practice is followed. The second course is moved inwards about half an inch to support the grate.

bottom: The grate is formed with six bricks about three inches apart to allow flow of air and fall of ash. The wall bricks are tight against the ends of the transverse bricks which form the grate.

right: The next two courses of
bricks are moved inwards half an
inch to support the roof of the
firebox and the floor of the firing
chamber.

226

top, bottom: Nine bricks form the roof of the firebox. After the sixth brick a space of two inches is left. A further space of three inches is made between the ninth brick and the rear wall. These last three bricks are, in effect, the floor of the firing chamber.

right, opposite: The door, which is
made up of two bricks is centred
in front of the three bricks which
form the floor of the firing chamber.
Two courses are laid around the
firing chamber as shown. A third
course is moved half an inch
inwards to support the roof of the
firing chamber. A space of two
inches by nine inches is left at the
rear of the roof to form the top
flue.

kiln furniture

Shelving can be made from fire clays and coarse high alumina grog. This is satis factory for low temperatures, but at stoneware temperatures the shelves must be o excellent quality not to warp. Silicon-carbide and sillimanite shelves are made for high temperatures. Sillimanite tends to warp after 1250°C. Special kiln furniture can be bought for plates and tiles, but it is not necessary for the small potter.

Spacing props between the shelves or 'bats' as they are known, can be thrown cylinders of fireclay and grog. Ready made spacing props are available from refractory suppliers. Firebrick can be cut. Insulating refractory brick is brittle and will not stand much weight without crumbling, but a stonemason or the refractory suppliers will cut firebricks into neat blocks.

Shelving is dusted with fine sand or silica for firing to prevent ware sticking.

A stiff mixture of sand and Kaolin will make good wadding between kiln props and shelves for secure setting.

heat measurement

Two main heat factors interest the potter. They are the rate of rise in temperature and the work it is doing. Some experienced potters fire only by the appearance of the kiln atmosphere and the ware. This takes time to learn, but once again the little Raku kiln can introduce the novice potter to judgment of maturity of ware with minor losses.

Most potters rely on some mechanical means of measuring heat. Various types of pyrometers are available which will measure the kiln temperature. These have a thermocouple, two wires made of dissimilar metals which are joined at one end which intrudes into the kiln. As they are heated a current is registered on a dial calibrated in degrees Centigrade and Fahrenheit. The thermocouple will eventually corrode at the joined end and need repair.

The cheapest variety, using chromel/alumel wire, is strong and it is recommended only for use to about 1100°C. Platinium/platinium-rhodium thermocouples and others made from similar more expensive metals will work over all the high temperatures used by the potter. When buying, consult the supplier for advice on this equipment.

The pyrometer measures the rate of rise in temperatures. When firing, the rate of climb can be observed to see if the firing is being done efficiently. The pyrometer does not show the work the heat has done, only the actual heat. So if a kiln has been fired quickly, the temperature decided upon may be reached but the ware will not have reached maturity. It will show cooling temperatures, after the cones are over, where special glaze effects are required.

Pyrometric cones are the commonest means used to gauge work heat. These cones are three sided pyramids of ceramic materials, designed to soften and bend at required temperatures. They are placed in special racks or small mounds of well grogged clay and are slightly tilted towards the direction they will fall, as indicated by the base when the cone is stood up. Three cones may be used in a kiln. The first is a warning cone, one cone number below the firing cone. When it bends, it indicates that the ware is approaching maturity. The second is the firing cone. When bent, it tells that the ware is fired to maturity. The third, or guard cone, must not fall or the fire will have been taken beyond the point decided on. This cone is one number higher than the firing cone.

There is a small variation in temperatures relative to the speed of firing the kiln. Take care to have the cones easily seen through the spy hole. Place them in the kiln where they will give a fair idea of the average work done in the whole kiln. Special glasses, such as those used in welding, may be worn during inspection of the kiln at high temperatures.

Other means of heat-work measurement are done by similar ceramic devices such as bars and the buller's rings, where the shrinkage of the ring is measured. The ring is hooked from the kiln during firing.

Optical radiation pyrometers can use the visible radiation of the ware in the kiln to measure temperature.

left: The appearance of three Pyrometric cones on completion of firing will indicate the effect of heat. In the foreground is the warning cone, in the centre the maturing cone and behind is the guard cone.

appendixes

glossary of terms
methods of measuring shrinkage
some raw materials and their use

a glossary of terms

ACID

The principal acid used in glazes is silica (S_1O_2) of the RO_2 group. It is used with the bases and the neutrals to make a glaze. Borax, also an acid, gives variety of colour.

AGEING

(Weathering) the storing of clay for a period allows bacterial and chemical reactions to take place, usually in a damp, warm environment, to improve the clay body.

ALKALI

Fluxing compounds:– Sodium, potassium and alkaline earths such as lime and magnesia.

ASH

Ash from grasses and trees is used to make stoneware glazes. Some ashes have the ingredients, although these are not balanced, to be almost a complete glaze within themselves.

ASYMMETRY

Shape and form distortion, with balance usually maintained.

BAG WALL

A wall behind the firebox to prevent direct flame impingement on the ware.

BAIT

To stoke a kiln.

BAT

A disc of material used as a base on which to throw or to dry pottery. Also a kiln shelf.

BINDERS

Substances used to adhere glazes to the body. Common glues such as gum arabic, gum tragacanth, dextrine and the synthetic resin range of glues.

BISQUE OR BISCUIT

Ware fired to a hard enough body to facilitate handling in glazing.

BLOWING

As the outer surface of the clay sinters during too rapid a rise in temperature in the kiln, steam trapped in the body expands and blows the ware to pieces.

BLUNGE

To mix clay thoroughly in a mechanical mixer.

BODY

A mixture of clays and non-plastics to form a satisfactory combination for working and firing.

BULLER'S RINGS

A trial ring which measures kiln heat by contraction.

BURNISHING

Rubbing the surface of the clay to cause the grains of clay to lie in such a fashion as to present a smooth and polished surface.

CALCINE

To heat a material to sufficient temperature to drive off chemical water and remove volatile matter to render it inert; usually about red heat 600°C.

CALLIPERS

Devices to measure the inside or outside diameters of pottery.

CASTING

Process of reproduction with liquid clay in Plaster of Paris or biscuit moulds.

CASTING SLIP

Clay which has been *deflocculated* (turned to a liquid) for casting in moulds.

CELADON GLAZE

Grey-green glaze produced by iron under reduction fire.

CENTRING

Using the pressure of the arms and the centrifugal forces of the wheel to bring a ball of clay to the centre of the wheel. Also tapping a leather-hard piece as it rotates on the wheel to move it to the centre.

CHATTER

A series of indents around a piece caused by turning a pot with a blunt or incorrectly held turning tool.

CHEMICAL WATER

(H_2O) Water chemically combined with the material being fired, which is driven off just prior to red heat.

CHUCK

A clay or plaster form used on the wheel or lathe to hold pottery while turning or decorating.

CLAMMING

Sealing kiln doors with sandy clay.

COILING

Forming pottery by the use of rolls of clay welded together.

COLLARING

Closing in the rim of a cylinder with both hands while throwing.

CONES

Three sided pyramids made of ceramic materials blended in such proportions as to cause them to bend at specific temperatures in kiln firing, thus recording the work done by the heat. The two main types are *Seger* and *Orton* cones which have slightly different maturing points.

CRACKLE

Controlled crazing of glaze for decorative effect.

CRAWLING

When the glaze is fired and retracts to expose the bare body. Caused by a glaze cracking after dipping, particularly double dipping or dirty surfaces.

CRAZING

(a) Cracking of the glaze caused by uneven tension between glaze and body during cooling. Sometimes long delayed.
(b) The mild expansion of a porous body, through hydration, causing body and glaze tension.

CROWN

The roof of a kiln.

CRYSTAL GLAZES

Iron, lime, zinc and rutile with alkaline glazes will usually cause crystalline structures in the glaze with slow cooling.

CUTTING WIRE

Any line, cord or wire used to cut the clay ware off a surface.

DAMPER

A ceramic or metal plate used to control the flow of gases in a flue to give the required atmosphere in a kiln.

DE-AIRING

Passing clay through a vacuum, while pugging, to remove all air from the clay. This process also gives instant plasticity otherwise attained by ageing.

DEFLOCCULENT

Minute quantities of sodium carbonate or sodium silicate, one third to one half per cent, used to cause clay to become a liquid when mixing with the minimum addition of water.

DEHYDRATION

Steaming or water smoking in the biscuit fire, removing water from the clay before red heat.

DEVITRIFICATION

The re-crystallization in glasses and glazes in the cooling process.

DIPPING

Glazing by immersion.

DRYFOOT

Ware cleaned of all glaze on and slightly above the foot.

DUNTING

Cracking of ware caused by too rapid cooling of the kiln.

DOWNDRAUGHT KILN

A kiln built in such a way that the hot gases pass up to the crown, thence down through the ware and the floor before being exhausted.

EARTHENWARE

Glazed porous ware fired below about 1200°C.

ENGOBE

A coating of slip clay applied to colour or texture the body.

EUTECTIC

The lowest melting mixture of two or more substances; this is lower than their individual melting points.

EXTRUSION

Plastic clay being forced from a pugmill.

FETTLING

Finishing the leather-hard or dry clay ware by removing unwanted surface marks.

FILLER

A non-plastic ingredient in clay to control shrinkage and drying.

FILTER PRESS

A device to press excess water from clay slurry to form plastic clay.

FIREBOX

The chamber where the combustion of the fuel takes place in a kiln.

FIRING

The burning of a kiln.

FLUES

The passage ways for the hot gases in a kiln.

FLUX

Any material which lowers the fusion point of any mixtures in which it is present.

FOOT

The base of a pot.

FRIT

Powdered material ground from specific parts of a glaze which has been melted, cooled and ground to form an ingredient in the glaze composition. Principally used to make soluble substances in the glaze insoluble.

GEL

To form a thick gelatinous mass.

GLAZE

An impervious vitreous (glassy) coating on pottery.

GLOST FIRING

Glaze firing.

GREEN WARE

Unfired pottery articles.

GROG

A ground mixture of fired clay.

GUM TRAGACANTH

A binder used with colour and glaze. Half an ounce is soaked in a quart of water overnight. It will then be found to be a jelly-like mass. Stir and leave all day, then stir again and it will be ready for use. Add a germicide to prevent bacteria forming.

HARD GLAZE

A glaze having a high melting point because of the quantity of silicia in it.

HEARTH

The floor of a kiln.

IMPERMEABLE

A body vitrified to a non-porous state.

INDUCED DRAUGHT

Draught forced into a kiln by a fan.

JIGGERING AND JOLLYING

A method of making repetition shapes usually plates and cups on the wheel with plaster moulds and profile presses.

KHAKI

Opaque rust-brown glaze.

KICK WHEEL

A throwing wheel rotated by the foot.

KIDNEY

A kidney shaped piece of flexible metal or rubber for finishing and smoothing clay.

KILN

The furnace or oven for firing pottery.

KNEADING

Mixing clay to a homogeneous texture by hand or foot.

LEATHER-HARD

Partially dry clay ware, still soft enough to turn or finish, but firm enough to handle without fear of distortion or damage.

LEVIGATION

Washing with water by carrying fine particles away from coarse.

LIME GLAZE

A glaze whose chief ingredient is calcium usually in the form of whiting.

LUG

Handle or knob.

LUTING

Joining clay pieces with slip.

MASTER MOULD

Mould from which production moulds are made.

MATT GLAZE

A glaze without a shiny surface.

MATURITY

The point of firing when the glaze and body reach the desired state of fusion and vitrification.

MEMORY OF CLAY

The return of clay to a previous shape from which it has been strained in the making.

MODULUS OF ELASTICITY

The ratio of stress and strain.

MUFFLE

An enclosed space in the kiln to prevent direct flame impingement on the ware.

NEGATIVE SPACE

That space which surrounds on object and explains its presence.

NEUTRAL ATMOSPHERE

An atmosphere in the kiln intermediate between reducing and oxidizing.

NON-PLASTICS

Materials which, when mixed with water, have no plasticity, such as feldspar, silica, grog and so on.

ONCE-FIRED WARE

Pottery glazed and fired in one firing.

OPACIFIERS

Materials added to a glaze to make it opaque.

OPENING MATERIAL

Non-plastics such as silica, grog and so on used to assist drying and reduce shrinkage.

ORTON CONES

Temperature cones used in the United States. The numbers do not coincide with *Seger Cones*.

OXIDE

Any element combined with oxygen.

OXIDATION OR OXIDIZING FIRE

To fire the kiln with an oxidizing atmosphere; to have an absence of carbon monoxide and an excess of air. Sufficient oxygen will assure this condition, resulting in a clean flame without soot or smoke.

PADDLING

Striking the clay form with a paddle shaped tool to thin the walls and shape the form.

PEELING

Flaking of the glaze when glaze is not under compression.

PITCHER

Finely ground fired pottery.

PLASTICITY

The condition which allows clay to be formed without cracking or crumbling.

PORCELAIN

Hard non-absorbent pottery, usually white or grey and translucent, fired between 1250 and 1450°C.

POROSITY

The quality of being able to absorb liquid into open pores.

PRIMARY CLAY

Clay decomposed from the original rock and still on the same site.

POSITIVE SPACE

That space which is contained by the form and/or gives it a function.

PRESS MOULDS

Moulds in two pieces, especially made with troughs around the form to take the excess clay while pressing a solid shape.

PYROMETER

An instrument for measuring high temperatures, either by measuring the minute electrical charge induced into two dissimilar metals, or by optical means. Used to give the rate of rising and falling temperature. The pyrometer gives an actual heat measurement, whereas the cone gives heat work performed. As the cone is already bent after maximum temperature is reached, it cannot show the falling temperature if this is required. The pyrometer can.

PYROMETRIC CONES

See cones.

PUGMILL

A mixer for plastic clay. The de-airing type has a vacuum chamber to remove air from the clay.

RAKU

Soft, heavily grogged, low fired earthenware, usually lead glazed. Today made in Japan for the tea ceremony. Raku variations are practised widely in the United States by art-potters.

RAW GLAZE

A glaze containing no fritted material.

RAW GLAZING

The glazing of unfired pottery, which is then fired only once.

REDUCTION

Condition in a kiln if not enough air is supplied to burn the carbon particles and compounds in the flame completely.

REDUCTION FIRING

Firing with a limited oxygen supply so that combustion is incomplete, causing a smoky fire and flame at the ports. Normally the process is begun about the time the glaze commences fluxing. The clay and glaze are robbed of part of their oxygen content, causing changes to colour and surface, such as copper red, and celadon type glazes.

REDUCING AGENT

A material such as silicon carbide which gives off carbon-monoxide during firing.

REFRACTORY

Materials having a resistance to heat, which will not melt below a very high temperature, and used for kiln building and furniture.

RIB

A tool for smoothing thrown ware.

RIM

The top edge of the pot.

SAGGAR

A refractory box in which to stack ware that needs protection from the flame.

SALT GLAZING

Using the vapours developed by salt when it is thrown into a hot kiln. The salt glaze covers the ware and all the inside of the kiln with a hard glassy surface.

SECONDARY CLAY

Clay transported from its original site by water or wind and deposited elsewhere. Red clays, ball clays and fire clays.

SEGER CONE

A pyramidal ceramic cone made to bend at a known temperature to record heat work performed.

SETTING

Placing ware in the kiln.

SGRAFFITO

A decorating technique. Incising through a layer of clay slip or glaze to reveal a different colour of clay or glaze below.

SHALE

Hard laminated clay.

SHARD

A broken piece of pottery

SHIVERING

Peeling of glaze, caused by compression of the glaze.

SHORT

Non-plastic.

SHRINKAGE

Contraction of clay in drying and firing.

SILICEOUS CLAY

Sandy clay or clay high in silica.

SINTERING

(a) The drawing together of clay particles when fired to attain cohesion but not fusion (b) The early maturing of a glaze.

SLAB POTTERY

Pottery constructed with clay slabs.

SLAKE

To soak in water.

SLIP

Liquid clay. A suspension of clay or glaze in water of ceramic consistency.

SLIP CASTING

Making pottery in moulds with deflocculated liquid clay.

SLIP GLAZE

A glaze made with a large percentage of clay.

SLURRY

A thin mixture of clay and water.

SMOKING

The slow preheating of ware in a kiln.

SOAK

To hold the kiln temperature at one point for the heat to evenly saturate all the ware.

SOLUBLE

Being capable of dissolving in water.

SPRIGGING

Applying relief decoration with moulded plastic clay.

STACK

To load a kiln with ware.

STAMPS

Pieces of wood, clay or plaster engraved with designs which are embossed on leather-hard clay.

STEAMING

The slow removal of water from the clay ware in the early stages of firing before red heat.

STILLIARDS OR STILLAGES

Racks to hold boards of ware.

STONEWARE POTTERY

Pottery which is opaque, hard and usually vitreous or non-porous, fired above 1200°C.

TEMMOKU

Black iron stoneware glaze (Japanese glaze description).

TERRA-COTTA

Low fired unglazed pottery.

THROWING

Using the momentum of the potter's wheel to draw plastic clay into various circular forms.

TRAILING

Decorating with slip from a syringe or similar trailer.

TRANSLUCENT

Allowing light to shine through, but not transparent.

TRANSMUTATION

In pottery to change colours by reduction in firing.

TURNING

Trimming pottery on the wheel while it is leather-hard.

TURNING TOOL

A tool to trim pottery on the wheel, usually a loop of wire or metal on a handle, or a sharpened edge at an angle to its handle.

UNDERGLAZE

Coloured decoration applied on the clay or biscuit ware before glazing.

UPDRAUGHT KILNS

Kilns in which the hot gases pass directly from the firebox through the ware and up through the chimney flue.

VISCOSITY

Used in pottery to define glazes which flow slowly.

VITREOUS

When pottery has fused into a non-porous, low absorbent, glassy hard mass.

VOLATIZATION

To turn from a solid to liquid to a gas in extreme heat. Particularly evident in salt glazing.

WAD

Open clay used to level shelves and seal saggars in kilns.

WATER GLASS

Sodium silicate. A deflocculent used in the making of casting slip.

WATER SMOKING

The removal of water from ware is divided into three periods. During the first, increasing heat drives mechanical water from the clay, because much remains after drying. Then hygroscopic water is removed at about 150°C. Then there remains the chemically held water which is integral in the clay particles. This commences to eliminate at about 400°C. and continues to about red heat. To this point the kiln should be fired slowly and carefully, with ample air passage. Once it has been reached, the rate of firing can be increased.

WAX RESIST

Wax applied during decorating to prevent further application of colour or glaze on that part.

WEATHERING

Exposing clay to the weather to improve its plasticity.

WEDGING

Cutting and striking clay forcibly to remove air and make the mass homogeneous.

WHEEL THROWN POTTERY

Pottery formed on a potter's wheel.

WICKET

Doorway to a kiln usually constructed of loose brickwork and clammed.

WIRE

Flexible wire or cord used to cut clay, or separate ware from the wheel or bat.

methods of
measuring shrinkage

DRYING SHRINKAGE

Per cent linear shrinkage equals

$$\frac{\text{Plastic Length} - \text{Dry Length}}{\text{Plastic Length}} \times 100$$

Per cent absorption equals

$$\frac{\text{Saturated weight} - \text{Dry weight}}{\text{Dry weight}} \times 100$$

FIRING SHRINKAGE

Per cent linear shrinkage equals

$$\frac{\text{Dry Length} - \text{Fired Length}}{\text{Dry Length}} \times 100$$

TOTAL SHRINKAGE

Per cent linear shrinkage equals

$$\frac{\text{Plastic length} - \text{Fired length}}{\text{Plastic length}} \times 100$$

approximate squatting
temperatures seger cones

DEGREES C.	DEGREES F.	SEGER CONE NO.
600	1112	022
650	1202	021
670	1238	020
690	1274	019
710	1310	018
730	1346	017
750	1382	016
790	1454	015a
815	1499	014a
835	1535	013a
855	1571	012a
880	1616	011a
900	1652	010a
920	1688	09a
940	1724	08a
960	1760	07a
980	1796	06a
1000	1832	05a
1020	1868	04a
1040	1904	03a
1060	1940	02a
1080	1976	01a
1100	2010	1a
1120	2048	2a
1140	2084	3a
1160	2120	4a
1180	2156	5a
1200	2192	6a
1230	2246	7
1250	2282	8
1280	2336	9
1300	2372	10
1320	2408	11
1350	2462	12

squatting temperatures
orton cones

CONE NO.	20°C RISE PER HOUR	15°C RISE PER HOUR
022	585	605
021	595	615
020	625	650
019	630	660
018	670	720
017	720	770
016	735	795
015	770	805
014	795	830
013	825	860
012	840	875
011	875	895
010	890	905
09	930	930
08	945	950
07	975	990
06	1005	1015
05	1030	1040
04	1050	1060
03	1080	1115
02	1095	1125
01	1110	1145
1	1125	1160
2	1135	1165
3	1145	1170
4	1165	1190
5	1180	1205
6	1190	1230
7	1210	1250
8	1225	1260
9	1250	1285
10	1260	1305
11	1285	1325
12	1310	1335
13	1350	1350

TEMPERATURE CONVERSION

$$(\text{Degrees Centigrade} + 40) \times \frac{9}{5} - 40 = \text{Degrees Fahrenheit.}$$

$$(\text{Degrees Fahrenheit} + 40) \times \frac{5}{9} - 40 = \text{Degrees Centigrade.}$$

some raw materials and their use

ALUMINA

(Al_2O_3) molecular weight 101.94 is introduced to pottery through clay and feldspar. It increases refractoriness and strength of clay bodies. It is used in most glazes.

BARIUM CARBONATE

($BaCO_3$), molecular weight 197.4, is used in glazes as a flux and to matt the surface. Some potters use barytes as a source of barium.

BENTONITE

Is used as a plasticizer in clay by an addition of up to 3 per cent in the clay body. In glazes, it acts as an adhesive to give stronger glaze bond and helps to prevent settling.

BORAX

($Na_2O: 2B_2O_3: 10H_2O$) molecular weight 381.43, is soluble in water. It is used as a flux in glazes, usually in a fritted form. It will alter the colour of some oxides.

CHROMIUM OXIDE

(Cr_2O_3), molecular weight 152, is used to give a green colour. Chrome turns brown in a zinc glaze. Tin tends to turn it pinkish.

CLAY

is the product of decomposed feldspathic rocks. The most important clays are the kaolinite group:– ($Al_2O_3 : 2SiO_2 : 2H_2O$) and the montmorillonite group:– ($MgCa$) $O : Al_2O_3 : 5SlO_2 : nH_2O$). Primary or residual clays are those found on their original site when rock is weathered into clay. One such clay is kaolin. Secondary clays such as ball clays and fire clays have been transported by water or wind. The microscopic plate-like structure of clay is thought to be responsible for its plasticity. The clay with the finest particles is the most plastic.

CLAY BALL

(Al_2O_3) : SiO_2 : $2H_2O$) molecular weight 258, is plastic fine grained sedimentary clay. It fires white to cream in colour, usually with a vitrifying range of cone 8 to cone 10. Ball clay often has an excessive drying shrinkage causing warping and cracking when used alone. But in a body it imparts plasticity.

CLAY, BENTONITE

($Al_2O_3 : 4SiO_2 : 9H_2O$) is an extremely plastic clay used in small quantities to improve the work-ability of a clay or for the adhesion and suspension of glazes.

CLAY, CHINA

(kaolin) ($Al_2O_3 : 2SiO_2 : 2H_2O$) is residual clay of a white burnt colour because of its comparative purity. It is used in glaze to provide alumina and silica. Although not very plastic, it withstands high temperatures. It is used with a glaze to cause mattness.

CLAY, SAGGAR

is open refractory clay, capable of repeated firings. It is used to make saggars for kilns.

CLAY SLIP

is liquid clay that will cover and fit the clay body, and fuse at the desired temperature to form a glass, giving a natural glaze.

COBALT OXIDE

(Co_2O_3) molecular weight 240.8, is used as a blue colouring medium. Very little is required.

COLEMANITE

($2CaO : 3B_2O_3 : 5H_2O$) is a natural source of borax. As it is practically insoluble, it can be used without fritting.

COPPER CARBONATE

($CuCO_3$) $Cu(OH)_2$ molecular weight 221.16, produces greens in oxidizing fire and reds in reducing. It is poisonous.

COPPER OXIDE

(CuO) molecular weight 79.6, gives green, turquoise and red.

DIATOMACEOUS EARTH

is the siliceous remains of the skeletons of *diatoms* (miscroscopic organisms). It is used for insulation in brick or powder form.

DOLOMITE

($CaCO_3$: $MgCO_3$ or $CaMg(CO_3)2$) introduces both calcium and magnesia. It is used as a flux. When added to glaze in quantity it gives interesting yellowish-tan effects.

FELDSPAR

(Potash Feldspar) (K_2O : Al_2O_3 : $6SiO_2$) is the most important flux in ceramic bodies and glazes. It acts as a non-plastic opener in the clay body before firing. Feldspathic rocks are the origin of clay, which is formed by their decomposition.

FERRIC OXIDE

See iron oxide.

FLINT

(SiO_2) is silica ground from flint pebbles. The term is also used to describe any quartz or silica sand.

ILMENITE

(TiO_2 : FeO) is a rich, warm brown mineral sand colorant.

IRON OXIDE

(Ferrous oxide) (FeO). (Ferric Oxide) (Fe_2O_3) is the most common colouring medium in stoneware giving tans and browns. When used in celadon glazes it gives greens and greenish-blues.

KAOLIN

See Clay, China.

LIME

(Calcium Oxide) (CaO). Molecular weight 56, is introduced to pottery bodies and glazes as whiting (calcium carbonate) and dolomite (calcium carbonate and magnesium carbonate). Whiting is used as a flux in glaze and helps to form a hard glaze.

MAGNESIUM CARBONATE

($MgCO_3$) molecular weight 84.3, acts as a refractory at low temperature, but becomes a flux at high temperature.

MAGNESIUM SULPHATE

(Epsom Salts) ($MgSO_4$) when added to glaze in small quantities keeps it in suspension.

MANGANESE OXIDE

(MnO_2) molecular weight 87, gives browns, purples and blacks.

NEPHELINE SYENITE

($K_2O : 3Na_2O : 4Al_2O_3 : 9SiO_2$) is similar to feldspar but lowers the firing temperature required. Very useful in glazes and clay bodies.

NICKEL OXIDE

(NiO) is used to vary other colours in glazes.

OPAX

is a commercial opacifier made from zircon.

PLASTER OF PARIS

(Calcium sulphate) ($CaSO_4 : \frac{1}{2}H_2O$) is a powder for mould making.

RUTILE

(TiO_2) is impure titanium oxide used to stain glazes tan and golden brown, sometimes changing to blue under reduction. It tends to matt the glaze when used in quantity.

SILICA

(SiO_2) is sand, silica, quartz and flint. In the body, it reduces drying and burning shrinkage and gives hardness and resistance to wear. As a non-plastic it aids drying, but lowers plasticity. Silica is the principal acid (RO_2 Group) and with fluxes it will form a glaze. In the glaze, it is the principal glass former. It will raise the fusion point and may help to cure crazing.

SILICON CARBIDE

(SiC) molecular weight 40.07 is used to make kiln furniture. When about 0.5 per cent is used with an alkaline glaze and copper, the carbon will reduce to assist in red transmutations.

SILLIMANITE

($Al_2O_3 : SiO_2$) is used to make kiln furniture.

SODIUM CARBONATE

(Soda Ash) (Na_2CO_3) is mainly used as a deflocculent, reducing the quantity of water needed to change the clay into liquid slip.

SODIUM SILICATE

($Na_2O : xSiO_2$) is used for the same purpose. From 0.2 per cent to 0.5 per cent of sodium carbonate and/or sodium silicate is used normally. The resultant cast ware is usually strong for handling.

SODIUM URANATE

(Uranium Yellow) ($Na_2O : UO_3$) gives a yellow hue.

TALC

($3MgO : 4SiO_2 : H_2O$) is a hydrous magnesium silicate. It is usually a white, greasy mineral, slightly plastic and in a clay body a cheap source of magnesia to act as a flux. It imparts qualities to resist thermal shock and acid attack. It is used in glazes to give a soft opaque matt surface, being viscous and stable.

TIN OXIDE

(Stannic Oxide) (SnO_2) molecular weight 150.7, is a strong opacifier. From one to two per cent improves gloss and lustre of a glaze. Five to seven per cent gives a white opaque glaze. Other colours are used to tint the glaze. They in turn are affected by the tin. (e.g. chrome gives pink, not green).

TITANIUM DIOXIDE

(TiO_2) molecular weight 79.9, gives unusual matt and textured surfaces when added to a glaze. It is used as an opacifier.

URANIUM OXIDE

(UO_3) molecular weight 286.14, gives yellow, brown colour. See Sodium Uranate.

VANADIUM PENTOXIDE

(V_2O_5) molecular weight 181.9, produces various grades of yellow. It burns out in reduction but will give yellow to blue-greens with cobalt oxide.

VERMICULITE

is used for insulation.

VOLCANIC ASH (PUMICE)

is about equal to seventy per cent orthoclase feldspar and thirty per cent flint, with iron content in a glaze.

WHITING

(Calcium Carbonate) ($CaCO_3$) molecular weight 100.09, is used in clay bodies as a flux. But for stoneware it is mainly a glaze ingredient. See Lime.

ZINC OXIDE

(ZnO) molecular weight 81.38, may be used as a base or an acid in a glaze depending on the glaze constitution. An average of ten per cent is common. Larger quantities of zinc cause crystalline effects in glazes. It modifies colours of other oxides.

ZIRCONIUM OXIDE

(ZrO_2) molecular weight 123.22, is insoluble in water. In the body zircon gives high thermal shock resistance. It can be substituted for clay, flint or feldspar in a porcelain body. It produces opacity in a glaze, needing a greater quantity than tin, usually ten per cent to fifteen per cent by addition. It increases hardness and stabilizes colour.

7897 738
720 3·80 '3